1916 SURRENDERS

CAPTAIN H. E. DE COURCY-WHEELER'S
EYEWITNESS ACCOUNT

Alex Findlater

Easter 2016

ALEX FINDLATER

1916 Surrenders
© Alex Findlater 2016
alex@findlaterbook.com

ISBN 978-0-9540744-9-4

The photographs on page 44 and 87 are reproduced
courtesy of the National Museum of Ireland. The extracts
from Captain de Courcy-Wheeler's Field Diary, and
photographs, from the de Courcy-Wheeler papers in the
National Library of Ireland, are reproduced courtesy of
the National Library of Ireland.

Edited by A. & A. Farmar

Produced by Dún Laoghaire-Rathdown County Council

Comhairle Contae County Council

Designed, printed and bound by Concept2Print

CONTENTS

FOREWORD

As we mark the centenary of the Easter Rising, *1916 Surrenders* offers something new and unique to the existing wealth of material relating to that seminal event. Compiled by Alex Findlater, the detailed narrative provides a fascinating insight into the actions, experiences and reflections of his grandfather, Captain Henry de Courcy-Wheeler, who found himself at the beating heart of that extraordinary and bloody week. In April 1916, the military officer was ordered to Dublin from the Curragh to report to Brigadier-General W. H. M. Lowe, General Officer Commanding Dublin Forces. He was to serve as Staff Captain to General Lowe during Easter Week.

Captain de Courcy-Wheeler took the surrender of James Connolly, Thomas MacDonagh, Michael Mallin and Countess Markievicz (who was his wife's cousin) and was present when Patrick Pearse, accompanied by Nurse Elizabeth O'Farrell, surrendered to General Lowe on 29th April:

> "At 2.30 pm Commandant General Pearse, Commander-in-Chief, surrendered to General Lowe accompanied by myself and his A.D.C. at the junction of Moore Street and Great Britain Street, and handed over his arms and military equipment. His sword and automatic repeating pistol in holster and pouch of ammunition and his canteen which contained two large onions were handed to me by Commandant General Pearse. His sword was retained by General Lowe."

Immediately after the Rising, the captain wrote up his impressions in an army-issue field notebook. His grandson surmises that this was partly to clarify his mind prior to the forthcoming courts martial. Years later, de Courcy-Wheeler used his original notes, some pages of which are reproduced in this book, to create a more formal account, initially written by hand and later in typed form. That account, with accompanying historical images, forms the basis for this new and fascinating publication.

Early in 2012, the Department of Arts Heritage and the Gaeltacht agreed to fund the compilation of the initial section of the Irish Life and Lore 1916 Rising Oral History Collection. While working on the project, my husband Maurice O'Keeffe and I were privileged to meet and record the memories of Dorothea Findlater, daughter of Captain Harry de Courcy-Wheeler and mother of Alex Findlater, the compiler of this book who was also recorded for the project.

Between the covers of this book may be found a most carefully crafted account by a military officer with first-hand experience of the surrenders in 1916. Generated from a source not generally mined for accounts of Easter Week, it offers a fresh perspective on, among other things, the demeanour of the surrendering leaders, the mood of the crowds and the battle-scarred face of Dublin. Also palpable in its pages is the sense of responsibility which weighed heavily on the captain's shoulders. The Rising and its contested legacy has been, and will continue to be, a matter for wide and exhaustive debate, but the primary source material in this publication will help to balance and broaden our understanding of that seminal moment in our history.

Jane O'Keeffe
February 2016
www.irishlifeandlore.com

PREFACE

Captain Harry de Courcy-Wheeler recorded in his Field notebook instructions given and received, and aides-memoires, while he was Staff Captain to General Lowe during the 1916 Rebellion, as he called it. From these rough notes he wrote up his account of the surrenders of Commandants Pearse, Connolly, Mallin, Markievicz and MacDonagh. At a later date he recorded a fuller account and it is this that is reproduced here. He also gave an account of his time as the Administrator in the Curragh Military Camp 1914–1919. This is complemented by his daughter Dorothea's recollections of her time there as a seven-year-old.

Harry's brother Billy, one of the foremost surgeons in the city at the time, tended to the wounded on both sides, on the streets and in the hospitals to which he was attached. There is a short account of his involvement.

The editor of the leading social magazine of the day, *The Lady of the House*, describes his experiences during the Rising in terms suitable for his middle-class south county Dublin readers. The journal was an imaginative partnership between the editor Crawford Hartnell and the Findlater organisation.

Harry was an enthusiastic amateur photographer and took some interesting photographs during the Rising, and later of the revolvers and pistols surrendered to him. These are shown, some for the first time, within the text.

The iconic photograph of Commandant General Pearse surrendering to General Lowe is examined as is the likelihood that it was Harry who took the picture. The Surrender Manifesto (there were a number of copies) is discussed and the one that sold for €700,000 in 2005 identified.

Harry was unable to get through to Boland's Mills to serve the Surrender Manifesto on Commandant de Valera. There is a short piece on his surrender.

Alex. Findlater & Co. in Upper Sackville Street (now O'Connell Street), occupied a large portion of the block opposite the Parnell Monument and survived undamaged: neither bombed, fired upon nor looted, notwithstanding the fact that it held one of the largest stocks of food in the city.

ACKNOWLEDGEMENTS

In 2013 Donal Byrne of RTÉ television interviewed my mother, Dorothea, on her memories of 1916 and life in the Curragh Military Camp during World War I. Her father was the Camp Administrator with a staff of seventy. She protested that she was only seven at the time and would have little to contribute, nevertheless she did them proud. Almost simultaneously Maurice and Jane O'Keeffe of Irish Life and Lore were compiling the 1916 Rising Oral History Collection and were keen to get her contribution. Her one-hour recording is now part of the National Collection available in the libraries throughout the country.

RTÉ were researching for 1916 centenary programmes and saw an opportunity in the surrender of Commandant Michael Mallin to Captain Harry de Courcy-Wheeler outside the College of Surgeons. They, and Irish Life and Lore, were able to interview two wonderful people who lived through those terrible events; first, Fr Joseph Mallin, the 103-year-old son of Michael Mallin, a retired missionary priest living in Hong Kong, and then Harry's 106-year-old daughter, Dorothea, here in Dublin.

Out of these interviews came this book. The search for fresh information unearthed the dictated and typed account of Captain de Courcy-Wheeler's part in the Rising, an earlier hand-written account and finally the faded microfilm record of his Field Notes jotted down as events unfolded. The National Library turned up trumps with hitherto unpublished photographs amongst the Wheeler papers.

To Donal Byrne and the RTÉ team, Maurice and Jane O'Keeffe, the Librarians in the National Library, the Curators in the National Museum, Geoff Shannon, Dr Horace de Courcy-Wheeler, George de Courcy-Wheeler and Grattan de Courcy-Wheeler, most sincere appreciation for access to records, cooperation, and the talents to enable this projects to reach viewers, listeners and readers.

Publications need a good management team and I was happy when Tony and Anna Farmar, publishers of *Findlater's—The Story of a Dublin Merchant Family 1774–2001*, agreed again to work on the manuscript. Thanks also to Dún Laoghaire-Rathdown County Council who offered to produce the book and include the launch in their series of 1916 events. Finally, the design and print have been ably undertaken by Richard Howlett and his team in Concept2Print. Again many thanks to all involved.

Alex Findlater, March 2016.

Sackville Street in the immediate aftermath of the Rising, showing the destruction caused by fire and by the shelling from the Navy gunship in the Liffey.

THE DESTRUCTION OF SACKVILLE STREET DUBLIN 1916
BY CRAWFORD HARTNELL

Crawford Hartnell was the Conductor (Editor) of the women's magazine The Lady of the House.[1] *In the first issue after the Rebellion, published on 15th May, he described his experiences and reactions during the Rising, in terms suitable for his middle-class, largely Protestant audience.*

WHEN I FIRST HEARD THE NEWS.

'What was the meaning of that quare business at the General Post Office to-day, Sir? I hear Larkin's army has seized it' said the conductor of the last Tram destined to run out of Dublin for ten days.

It was Easter Monday, and having gone up to Town I was hurrying home to lunch, and just as I descended from the car these words of the Conductor, who knew me as a daily passenger, brought the first tidings of the insurrection.

It was then 1 o'clock and the environs of Dublin, bathed in brilliant sunshine and looking their loveliest, were filled to overflowing with excursionists. These had come to the seaside by the early trains and were destined to trudge many weary miles back to the City, footsore and wretched, with worn out, fagged, bedraggled children, clinging to their hands, or their garments, for the splendid railway accommodation, like the admirable tramway service, had mysteriously ceased. The city was completely cut off from its immediate environs, still a message could be got through. I went to the Post Office to find that the wire was not working: I sought the Telephone Call Office and there was no communication. Meanwhile rumour wagged her pivoted hundred tongues, dripping with horrors, as though the joint resurrection of Ananias and Edgar Allan Poe had come to pass and the pair had resumed their life-work in partnership.

THE HATCHING OF AN INSURRECTION.

It was the following morning, Easter Tuesday, before I had the chance of investigating matters at first hand. I drove to Ball's Bridge and looked in at the fine Spring Show of the Royal Dublin Society. Some hundreds of the beasts for exhibition had not arrived, having been held up in transit. I next drove on to the City and called into the offices of *The Irish Times,* where the belated issue for the day, censored literally to death, was coming from the machines. Meeting one of the Directors of Messrs. Eason, Ltd., who was staying at the Metropole Hotel to be near his concerns during the critical times, I volunteered to walk with him up Sackville Street [now O'Connell Street, as Nationalists had called it since 1884] so that I might observe the trend of affairs for myself. As a witty man observed 'It was Sackville Street with the accent on the *sack.*'

THE FRENCH REVOLUTION IN MINIATURE.

Sackville Street was crowded, and the worst of the slum population— the wretched folk who inhabit the tenements formed of the old mansions of the dead and gone, or emigrated, aristocracy—were about in great and quite unusual force. The corner houses, with one or two exceptions, showed piled up sandbags in their windows arranged for defensive purposes. Over the General Post Office floated two flags, one a green, white and orange tricolour, the Larkinite colours, and near the Portico the Proclamation of the 'Irish Republic' was posted. Across Lower Abbey Street a barricade was thrown, built of furniture, carts, bicycles, barrels, reels of paper, taken from the emergency office of *The Irish Times,* nearby.

From or about this barricade and elsewhere, continuous objectless firing came, and I saw a boy struck in the temple and brought off, blood spouting from his wound. A filthy gutter-snipe with an old fowling piece was menacing an aged man, and a few steps further a dirty unwashed woman of the slums, ragged and unkempt, with her matted hair surmounted by a fashionable hat—probably three guineas worth—shuffled past, her dirty naked feet thrust into fashionable patent leather shoes. The source of these fineries was not far to seek, for the pavement was ankle deep in finely broken plate glass, shattered by blows, in order to place the shopkeeper's stock at the mercy of the itching fingers from the slums. A bundle of rags without shoes—strange that anyone should be in that condition, for almost every boot shop in Sackville Street had paid toll and boots were to be had for four pence a pair—still this particular bundle of rags, a male bundle, had other tastes and had gratified them, for under one arm he held a valuable clock and under the other a working model of a steamship, evidently a costly toy from Mr. William Lawrence's establishment, then looted, shortly to be burnt down.

The thieves and bad characters of Dublin swarmed from their dens into Sackville Street just as those of London had invaded Regent Street in the days of the Dockers' strike, and those of Belfast had attacked the shops in the riots of the sixties. These are the dirty fringes that hang upon the mantle of disorder. Some of the insurrectionists endeavoured in many cases to stop the thieves, but their action had liberated a force which they were powerless to control.

What a scene! Had I been a photographic plate, exposed in Sackville Street that Easter Tuesday morning I could have presented one phase of the French Revolution in miniature.

I passed back across Town to College Green where Trinity was occupied by the military, who had filled the windows with sandbags. The great gates were closed, and within a Parliamentary election was in progress, for Mr. J. H. Campbell, our new Attorney-General, one of the gentlemen who started the present Volunteering and arming in Ireland, was being elected for the 'Borough of the College', one of the few James 1st Boroughs, which survived the Union.

The Bank of Ireland, the old Parliament House, also was closed, and during the whole insurrection no one ever tapped at its doors.

YPRES ON THE LIFFEY.

Sackville was one of the four great streets in Europe. It was one of the chief gems of the beautiful classic city of Dublin. I had seen it for the last time on Easter Tuesday, and it was not until the following Friday that I was destined to look upon its site again. I had walked with a friend from Ball's Bridge to Merrion Row, via Pembroke Road and Baggot Street, and had heard the whirr of the machine guns from St Stephen's Green, where testimony is borne to their activities by the hammered stone work of the beautiful facade of the Royal College of Surgeons—built, by the way, in part, on the site of the house wherein a former Dublin revolutionist, hapless Robert Emmet, was born.

The fine Shelbourne Hotel, held by the military, showed a few broken windows, but little other damage. The machine guns were worked from the top bedroom windows of the hotel against the College of Surgeons, the garrison of the latter relying on rifle fire.

Inside 'the Green' on the North side a series of shallow holes had been burrowed, the roots of the trees having prevented the digging of regular trenches, but at the South side better trenches existed, and these were made comfortable with cushions taken from the tramway cars held up on the rails outside. From and about 'the Green', the dead bodies of some seven insurgents had been removed that morning in the carts commandeered from a local manufacturer. Nor were human dead the only sacrifices. At the eastern corner lay the remains of a dead horse—which, under the sun, had become so offensive that the windows of houses in the immediate vicinity, could not be opened for days, and on the western side, facing the Royal College of Surgeons, and tossed into the channel, was the body of a beautiful thoroughbred Irish terrier dog, shot through the heart, its red coat dabbled with its blood.

From Merrion Row to St. Andrew Street I did not meet one civilian, but in the distance, across Merrion Square, surgeons, in their white operating coats, and Red Cross nurses, flitted hither and thither. All along Lower Mount Street, Clare Street, Nassau Street soldiers were posted singly at every thirty yards. At the street corners soldiers lay prone on their waterproof sheets, nursing their rifles and intently watching the roofs, eaves and chimneys of the houses for snipers. My 'pass' was inspected at every corner, and I finally halted at the corner of Church Lane. 'You can go to the left, not to the right,' said the sentry. 'Why?' Well, the fact was that a house to house search was in progress and Dame Street was closed, but might be open in an hour. Two young girls stood in a doorway and could not go to their homes—a few doors around the corner to the right—until the embargo was removed.

That morning Blackrock was full of the news that Messrs. Switzers fine warehouses had been burnt to the ground. I would turn through Wicklow Street—a left turn—and so reach Grafton Street and inspect the ruins. So I went, to find, to my joy that Messrs. Switzers had not even a blister on its paint. One would have thought that, with horror on horror's head accumulating, the Ananias-Poe combination would have been overborne by the tragedy of hard fact. But no. The supposed fire at Messrs. Switzers was only one of a thousand fantasies such as the destruction of Messrs. Jacobs' biscuit factory and the murder of Lord Dunraven. Suburbia, indeed, assembled at the corners of the roads and almost frightened itself into imbecility with imaginary happenings.

Back to the corner of Trinity Street to see a squad of four formidable looking hooligan looters, marched under guard, down Dame Street in the direction of Dublin Castle, and in a few moments an obliging Second Lieutenant consented to convey me across Dame Street, which, save for the military, was quite deserted. After some delay at my offices I passed on *via* Anglesea Street to Fleet Street. In both thoroughfares military searches were being carried out, three men entering each house and turning out all the inhabitants, men, women and children, who were ordered to the other side of the street, and ranged against the wall, while their houses were searched. On again, down almost to Westmoreland Street—'Halt, your pass,' challenged a Sergeant. The order was instantly obeyed. 'Where are you going?' 'Across Westmoreland Street' 'Impossible—it is the danger zone.' I stuck to my point, and the man brought me to his Officer. 'Did I really want to go?' 'Yes' and the reason was explained. 'Oh, very well'. The word of command was given and four men stepped out and formed a square. I was placed in the centre, and the Officer came to my right-hand side. The order to march was given and we passed out of Fleet Street into the fire zone. As we approached the eastern side of Westmoreland Street the Officer addressed me. 'Look' said he, and I turned my head to the left and received the surprise of my life. The great thoroughfare had been bombed by the military, who began to arrive in force at Kingstown on Wednesday morning.

From O'Connell Bridge, at the lower end of Sackville Street, to the North side of Cathedral Street, above Nelson's Pillar there were only two objects, the facade of the Dublin Bread Company's premises and the shell of Messrs. Clery's splendid building. The rest was ruin, ashes, desolation. The air was thick with dust and smoke, fires burnt and smouldered everywhere. Through the smoke the flash-flash of the rifle—and there was much noise. Above all towered the figure of O'Connell, wrapped in his great cloak and seemingly in the attitude of one pronouncing a benediction. One spot was clear, and through it I saw the lovely portico of Francis Johnston's beautiful Post Office. 'I am glad that fine old building has been spared' said I to the Officer 'It will not be spared long' he replied. I had seen the Ypres of the 'Pictures' translated into a living reality. Alas that the translation should have been accomplished in my beautiful native city of Eblana.

I passed in to the Eastern portion of Fleet Street, and having accomplished my purpose returned across Westmoreland Street, I thanked the courteous Officer for the trouble he had taken. 'Not at all,' said he quite dryly. 'No trouble at all, you were a protection to us in fact, *for they hesitate to fire on us when we are escorting a prisoner.*' It was my *debut* as a military escort.

THE REBELLION AND JOURNALISM.

What was domestic life like in Dublin during the terror? Well, between Easter Monday and the 3rd of May no trams ran and few newspapers were published. *The Irish Times* missed publication on two days—28th and 29th April—when no daily newspapers were issued in Dublin, because the circulation of a paper was a physical impossibility, the *Independent* six days, because of the failure of power owing to the cutting off of the public gas supply; the *Freeman's Journal* seven days, for its offices were burnt down; and the *Daily Express* six days, because its high constitutional headquarters, facing the City Hall and Upper Castle Yard, were held as 'a fort' by the insurgents.

DOMESTIC INCONVENIENCES.

To return to our domestic inconveniences, no trains ran, no letters were delivered or forwarded, no telegrams were sent and no telephone messages were possible. The very coffins, containing the dead, were opened and inspected, on their last journey to the cemeteries, lest arms might be conveyed to the outskirts of the city, hidden in these grim receptacles. Housekeeping was a difficult matter, supplies were very short and prices were climbing up daily. Staid gentlemen were wandering about, with the mien of conquerors, the cause of their triumph being the couple of loaves tucked beneath their arms. Bread without butter was, however, a dry morsel and butter was costly. I heard of one conscientious trader in Pembroke district who actually charged six shillings for his butter, but that extortion was happily quite exceptional. Still the cost was sufficiently great and the stress severe.

No police were in the streets and there was no gas. I met a working man—an employee from the Tramway Power House at Ringsend and he assured me that he had thirty-five shillings in his pocket and was literally starving. I also chatter with a military veteran, not a Dublin man, who wore the ribbons of three medals, 'I have learnt one thing in Dublin, sir' said he 'and that is that the women and children of Dublin men, who are fighting in the trenches in Flanders, are starving in Dublin back streets because food is unobtainable, and this is strange, as on the march from Kingstown to Dublin we were given lots of food and tea, cigarettes and fruit, while we had plenty of good food of our own.'

STREET PASSES.

At first no person could move about without a military 'pass,' and these were often difficult to obtain. The 'passes' were issued at the Town Halls of Kingstown, Pembroke, Blackrock, etc.; Dublin Castle, Trinity College, and other centres, and people often waited in queues for hours and were unsuccessful in obtaining the permit. Cars and vehicles were stopped and searched. I was driving on an outside car over Baggot Street Bridge and had to get down, so that the newly landed sentries, who had never seen an outside car before in their lives, might search the vehicle. This they did by looking under the cushions, under the wing and behind the driver's legs. When they had finished, I introduced them to the 'well' of the car, the natural place of concealment, and the sentries gaped at me in unaffected astonishment. 'It bates all,' was the comment of the driver. I think he had the sentries' want of understanding of the possibilities of 'the car' in his mind.

Early in Easter week no person was permitted to be abroad in the streets of Dublin, 'pass' or no pass, after 7.30 p.m., and later on the hour was extended to 8.30. All the Theatres and other places of amusement were perforce closed, consequently, for the first time in its long and brilliant association with Dublin, the D'Oyley Carte Operas did not crowd the Gaiety Theatre.

THE DWELLING-HOUSE AS A 'FORT'

The real danger to the householder was the risk of his house being seized and used as a 'fort,' as so many houses were. When this seizure occurred late at night the unfortunate householder had often no place of refuge for himself and his family, save the dangerous streets. To remain in his home was to share the perils of the defence, to brave the fires which rose when the military 'bombed' the house, and should this occur, the grave risk of death, when the householder and his family were driven out by the conflagration, in company with the insurgents, to face the fire of the soldiers' rifles.

Through the outskirts of Dublin there are many fine houses, dismantled 'forts,' which are either burned down or cut to ribbons by rifle and machine gun fire. Nor is this the only revolution in the appearance of the city and suburban mansions, for almost every empty house has been taken as quarters by the military, and for the first time in my life I have seen men's underclothing, fresh from the wash tub, hung out to dry from the windows of the stately houses of Merrion Square.

THE LADIES, GOD BLESS THEM!

The Sherwood Foresters were the first regiment disembarked at Kingstown. They marched to Dublin, and after a brief rest at Ball's Bridge Showyard, crossed the Bridge and passed along Northumberland Road to Mount Street Bridge, where they were received by a terrible frontal fire, directed from Clanwilliam House, and a flank fire from both sides of the road. Seventy men fell, and like magic, in that zone of death, a body of veritable ministering angels—Nurses from Sir Patrick Dun's Hospital, who were resting at the Nursing Home in Lower Mount Street—crossed the Bridge and under fire attended the wounded. The Victoria Cross is not a decoration which falls to the lot of women, but these noble Dublin ladies, who knew no fear, deserved the highest honour man can bestow upon their noble courage and unfaltering devotion. These fine Dublin girls were worthy sisters of the brave men of the gallant Royal Dublin Fusiliers!

A GRIM RECOLLECTION

I write these hurried notes on Saturday, 6th May. Just thirty-four years ago, on another Saturday and on another 6th May, how well I remember the terrible convulsion that shook Dublin when the Phoenix Park murders stained the fair fame of the stately capital. There is no parallel between the Insurrectionists of 1916 and the Invincibles of 1886, but death, shame, tears, bloodshed, sorrow and ruin on both occasions attended the acts of those who engineered these two catastrophes. The motto of our city is a wise one: 'The Obedience of the Citizen is the greatest safety of the City.' When will we learn to lay that motto to heart and translate into action the wisdom of its teaching?

One last word as to the Insurrectionists. I saw fifty or sixty of them marched as prisoners up Dame Street to Dublin Castle. They were a fine body of young countrymen, decently attired, stalwart young fellows, who held themselves well and marched with elan, like well-drilled, soldierly men. They compare in appearance and mien more than favourably with their military guards. Only one was in uniform—a postman—wearing the livery of the Postal Service. They bore themselves stoically as men who had hazarded and lost and were prepared to pay the penalty. That, I think, was the saddest sight of all that I had seen during these terrible days.

The Lady of the House was founded in 1890 as 'The Only Fashion Journal in Ireland'. It was non-sectarian and non-political, but generally progressive. It supported women in education, in business and the professions and in sport (especially bicycling) but tactfully remained silent on the divisive issue of voting rights.

In the Spring issue, March 1891, under 'Circulation' it said: 'Twenty Thousand Copies of this number of the '*Lady of the House*' have been published. This circulation, which is more than double that of any Irish Periodical, is attested by sworn certificate'.

The journal was an imaginative partnership between Crawford Hartnell and Findlater's. It was published by Wilson, Hartnell who later became one of Ireland's leading advertising agencies. In 1909 Findlater's agreed a considerable advertising schedule and to purchase 3,000 copies monthly at sixpence per dozen copies.

Hartnell, who referred to himself as 'The Conductor', undertook that the literary tone and character of the periodical, and the printing, paper and illustrations would be of a style and character not inferior to that of the issues of the twelve months preceding the agreement. It had a sister publication *Findlater's Ladies Housekeeping Diary*. In 1931 *The Lady of the House* amalgamated with *The Irish Tatler* and became *The Irish Tatler & Sketch*.

CAPTAIN HARRY DE COURCY-WHEELER — THE MAN

The author of the account of the 1916 surrenders that follows is my grandfather, Henry Eliardo de Courcy-Wheeler, known as Harry, and in the text abbreviated to H. E. de C.-W. He was born on St Patrick's Day, 17 March 1874, and lived a full life, dying aged 84 in December 1956.

His grandfather was George Nelson Wheeler. He met a tragic end on the Bog of Allen while shooting game with a muzzle-loading hammer. He fired once and the gunpowder failed to ignite. He then looked down the barrel to see what was going on, and boom, off went his head! No doubt this taught Harry to treat firearms with respect.

His father, William Ireland Wheeler, was a celebrated surgeon and President of the Royal College of Surgeons in its Centenary year 1884. He was the first of a long line of doctors and surgeons in the family, eight in total. Harry was the second eldest son in a family of six sons and four daughters. He qualified as a Barrister-at-Law King's Inns in 1896 and graduated from TCD with an MA in Classics in 1903. In the same year he married Selina Knox, youngest daughter of Hercules Knox of Rappa Castle, Co. Mayo. They settled in Robertstown, Co. Kildare. He was an accomplished horseman and won the High Stone Wall Championship in the RDS.

On 9 May 1949 the *Evening Herald* reported that he was the only man to have won two first prizes while a practising member of the Bar with a busy practice on the Leinster Circuit. In 1904 he rode his 'fine little horse Sportsman', who stood 14.2", twice to victory, the second time in the Championship jumping event, open only to prize-winners in the previous competitions of the Show.

At the outbreak of World War I he became a Special Reserve Officer with the King's Royal Rifle Corps. He said that 'The advent of the first flying machine made me crazy with enthusiasm' to join the Royal Flying Corps to help save the Belgians. He underwent trials doing all sorts of stunts and was recommended but his application was blocked, probably because he was indispensable as Officer-in-charge of Barracks in the Curragh Military Camp.

In August 1914 he was ordered to join his regiment in England. In Robertstown the local company of the National Volunteers (the supporters of John Redmond), and the whole village, turned out to see him off. They presented him with a testimonial assuring him that his family and property would be safe in their hands until his return. This happened sooner than expected. On arriving in Dublin he received a

Henry Eliardo de Courcy-Wheeler, Barrister at Law, Robertstown House, Co. Kildare; born St Patrick's Day, 17th March 1872; married Selina Knox from Sligo, 19th April 1904; Administrator Curragh Military Camp World War I; Staff Captain to General Lowe during 1916 Rebellion; died aged 84, 13th December 1956.

telegram from the War Office in London ordering him back to his post in the Curragh. For the duration of the war he was the Administrator with a staff of seventy.

In April 1916 he was ordered to Dublin to report to General Lowe, general officer commanding the British forces in Ireland, to be his Staff Officer during the Rebellion. It was his experience as a member of the Bar and a Magistrate that brought him to the attention of the General.

After the Rising he returned to the Curragh and was there until he left the army in 1919 with the rank of Major. He did not enjoy legal work as, he said, he did not like defending criminals!

He was overcome with grief when Selina died in 1928, as a result of blow from a hockey ball a few months earlier. The *Sports Mail*, Saturday 25 February 1928, reported: 'A very regrettable accident happened on Monday last. Mrs de C.-W., who got a bad knock from a rising ball, was forced to seek surgical aid."

He was a good family man, an unenthusiastic farmer, a Greek and Latin scholar, an accomplished pianist, a talented horseman and was reluctantly caught up in a situation against his fellow countrymen whom he treated with dignity and respect. One of those who surrendered put it simply: 'The officer who took the surrender seemed a very decent sort of fellow. I think he was a Captain. I was just standing at the end of the line and he came along and looks at me, you know, and he gives me a clip on the ear and tells me to get the hell out of it.'

He was not a bit commercial in the running of the estate. He had a number of tenants on the land and every Friday he would receive the rent, 10d per week or whatever it was. He was fair handed in his dealings. When a tenant paid his rent, Harry would give him a bottle of stout. Of course there were occasions when the tenant came in and said: 'We haven't got the money this week, can we come back next week and pay?' To which Harry would reply: 'Of course you can, and here, have a bottle of beer!' The price of the rent was 10d and the value of the bottle of beer 6d!

By 1932 funds had dried up and the house and farm had to be sold. He settled in 'The Gables', Foxrock, (a large two-storey apartment over Findlater's premises) and immersed himself in his academic pursuits. He enjoyed genealogy, playing the piano and undertaking research such as trying to prove that it was Sir Francis Bacon who wrote William Shakespeare's plays and that an oil painting hanging on his wall should be reattributed to Vermeer! He held senior positions in the Masonic Order and would have been frequently in their establishment in Molesworth Street. He was fondly known as the Major and used the Royal Irish Automobile Club as his Dublin base, meeting his contemporaries there for convivial lunches at the Members' table. He travelled in and out on the Harcourt Street line, the Foxrock station being virtually on his doorstep. He passed away in 1956 at the age of 84.

During the Rising, H. E. de C-W had with him an army issue Field notebook, called the Field Message Book, in which he recorded orders given and received, aides-memoires and events as they happened; this so that he could accurately report to his commanding officers, and if called upon, refer to it at the courts-martial. After the Rising he used these notes to write up the events, first in his own hand, and years later a fuller account hand-written and typed. The latter appear in the following pages together with extracts from his field notes.

To Commandant
College of Surgeons.
The bearer of flag of truce
is authorised to instruct
you to leave down your
arms in Front Hall of
College & march out in single
file, and form up in front
of the College. H E de C Wheeler
Staff officer to
G.O.C. troops Dublin
30 Ap. 1916

Immediately after the events of the Rising, probably between then and the Courts martial, H. E. de C.-W. wrote up his Easter Week experiences in a standard issue Field Message Book. Years later he composed a fair copy which he had typed. This is the copy of a note from the Field Message Book that was to be carried under flag of truce by Nurse O'Farrell to Michael Mallin and the College of Surgeons garrison, instructing them how to surrender.

At the outbreak of the Irish Rebellion on Easter Monday the 24th April 1916 I was stationed on the Curragh.

By Tuesday the 25th April 1916 all the available troops had left there by road or had been entrained at the Curragh Siding for Kingsbridge, and were under the Command of Brigadier General W.H.M. Lowe, C.B. who was appointed General Officer Commanding the troops engaged against the rebels in the Dublin Area.

On the 28th April General Sir John Maxwell, K.C.B., K.C.M.G. C.V.O., D.S.O. arrived in Ireland with plenary powers from the British Government, and was appointed General Officer Commanding-in-Chief the Forces in Ireland.

On the 28th April at 10.30 p.m. I received an order through the Garrison Adjutant to report immediately to General Lowe's staff at Headquarters Irish Command Park Gate Street. I got my kit ready, borrowed a loaded revolver, overhauled my motor car and left the Curragh alone as the old water-Tower clock was clanking midnight. The journey was uneventful, the roads being totally deserted until I was close to Island Bridge. The houses from there to Parkgate seem to have been occupied by the British Military as I was suddenly pulled up with the cry of "Halt or I fire," all along the line, and when the car stopped a rifle with fixed bayonet was thrust through the window, the password demanded and information as to my identity and destination. I said "if you take that b——————— bayonet away from my chest I will be able to give you the information you want." I then showed the Sentry my instructions and he told me the way to reach Headquarters. From that point the whole City seemed to be in a blaze and rifle fire was going on in all directions and shells were bursting at intervals. However, there was no time to investigate, and I arrived at my destination at 1.45 a.m. The General and his staff had their Quarters in two adjoining rooms and were sleeping on the floor dressed in their uniforms. The telephone was going continuously and one of the staff Officers asked me to take it over as they had had no rest for three nights.

F.N. 54541
cal.
7.65 mm. Repeating Pistol in leather case pouch & ammunition belonging to General Pearse and handed to me by him when he surrendered in house Shut to General Lowe in 1916

H Ede C Wheeler

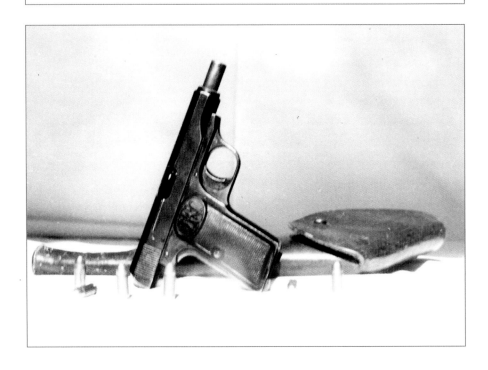

Pearse's repeating pistol

All sorts of messages came through as to the disposition of
troops, asking for orders, reports of snipers located in
various and distant parts of the city, houses blown up and
fires here, there, and everywhere, especially in Sackville
Street and the neighbouring Streets. One message I recollect
very distinctly, the Manager of a Bank in Upper Sackville
Street telephoned that the Bank was on fire, that there was a
Caretaker with a large family in the house and how were they to
escape. Upper and Lower Sackville Street were being swept with
rifle fire by snipers and the British Military were replying.
I asked the General what was to be done about this family en-
trapped in the burning Bank, and he said "tell them to march
out with a white flag." I 'phoned the Manager these instructions. Presently the telephone rang again from the Manager to
say they had no white flag and "would a Union Jack do?" That
put the lid on it. So I advised him to be quick and to make
a white flag or they would all be burned or shot! As I said,
the telephone kept going continuously all night until 11.30 a.m.
when I was relieved, and although I had taken charge of it, my
brother Officers got little rest. In the morning, one of the
General's Orderlies brought us a cup of tea and bread and butter
but a very limited supply, as rations were very uncertain and
few and far between. We had to go to Kingsbridge Station to
get something to eat and to Ross's Hotel near the Bridge.

At 12.30 information arrived that a Red Cross
Nurse was waiting at the Parnell Monument who had been sent by
Commandant Pearse to negotiate terms of surrender. The General
ordered me to accompnay him. It was a difficult matter at that
time to reach Parnell Monument from Headquarters Irish Command
in Parkgate Street, and it necessitated a zigzag course in and
out of side Streets and taking the intervening corners at high
speed owing to the sharp-shooters who were posted at vantage
points on the roofs of the houses; two bullets did get the

Pouch and ammunition belonging to Pearse

panel of the near door of the car, which was an Official Saloon car supplied for the use of the Staff, but owing to the skilful driver and the speed, I expect the snipers did not realise who was in it until it had skidded round the next corner.

Eventually the General and myself arrived at a small Newsagent's shop a few doors from the corner of Great Britain Street, where it joins Upper Sackville Street at the Parnell Mamment, and I was afterwards informed that this shop belonged to Mr. Tom Clarke, one of the seven Signatories to the Republican Proclamation. The General communicated the terms to the Sinn Fein Nurse, and she was allowed half-an-hour to return with the reply from Commandant General Pearse, who was in Command at the rere of the G.P.O. and controlled Moore Street and the adjoining thorough-fares. Upper Sackville Street was still swept by Snipers, and while waiting for the return of the Sinn Fein Nurse, General Lowe who was in his Staff Uniform, and a very conspicuous mark, strolled into Sackville Street to note the position. The whole of Upper and Lower Sackville Street was held by the Rebels at this time, and I felt responsible for the General's safety, and pointed out that he would draw the fire on himself if spotted. He made little of it, but in the end I persuaded him to return to the Newsagent's shop, and wait there for the despatches from the Rebel Commander-in-Chief. Soon after the Sinn Fein Nurse returned with a reply imposing conditions. These were refused, and the General sent her again to say that only unconditional surrender would be accepted, and that she could have half-an-hour to return with the reply.

At 2.30 p.m. Commandant General Pearse, Commander-in-Chief, surrendered to General Lowe accompanied by myself and his A.D.C. at the junction of Moore Street and Great Britain Street, and handed over his arms and military equipment. His sword and automatic repeating pistol in holster with pouch of ammunition and his canteen which contained two large onions were handed to me by Commandant General Pearse. His sword was retained by the General. The other articles are reproduced in the photograph.

In order to prevent the further slaughter of Dublin.
citizens, and in the hope of saving the lives of our
followers now surrounded and hopelessly outnumbered, the
members of the Provisional Government present at Head-
Quarters have agreed to an unconditional surrender, and the
Commandants of the various districts in the City and Country
will order their commands to lay down arms.

P. H. Pearse

29th April 1916
3.45 p.m.

I agree to these conditions for the men only under my own Command in the Moore Street District and for the men in the Stephen's Green Command.

James Connolly
April 29/16

On consultation with Commandant Ceannt and other officers I have decided to agree to unconditional surrender also

Thomas MacDonagh.

The original surrender document dated 29 April is in the Imperial War Museum in London.
This is a copy of it. Missing above after MacDonagh's signature is the date and time
written in by him: 30.1V.1916 3.15 pm. The handwriting above Connolly's signature is that
of H. E. de C.-W. See Appendix 5 for a detailed discussion.

There were two Army Official Motor cars waiting. Commandant General
Pearse accompanied by the General's A.D.C. was driven in the
General's Car, preceded by the General and myself in the other car
to Headquarters Irish Command to interview General Sir John Maxwell,
the British Commander-in-Chief.   After the interview Commandant
Pearse signed several typed copies of his manifesto, which was dated
by himself, Dublin, 29th April, 1916, and reads as follows :

      "In order to prevent the further slaughter of Dublin

    "citizens, and in the hope of saving the lives of our

    "followers now surrounded and hopelessly out-numbered,

    "the members of the Provisional Governments present at

    "Headquarters, have agreed to an unconditional surrender,

    "and the Commandants of the various districts in the city

    "and country will order their Commands to lay down arms."

After signing these documents Commandant General Pearse was con-
ducted to a sitting-room at Headquarters, I was ordered to keep
guard over him, and was locked in the room alone with Commandant
Pearse.   I was handed a loaded revolver with orders to keep it
pointed at Commandant Pearse, and to shoot should he make an effort
to escape.   This was a very responsible and serious order to obey
and to carry out should it have become necessary, but Pearse did
not seem in the least perturbed and greatly to my relief I was on
this duty for only fifteen minutes when I was sent for by General
Lowe and another Officer was sent to relieve me.   He ordered me
to go at once to the Castle, show the manifesto of Commandant
General Pearse, the Commander-in-Chief, to Commandant Connolly in
Command of the Irish Citizen Army who had been brought in wounded
and a prisoner, and get him to sign the document or a similar Order
to his own men.   When I arrived at the Castle, part of which had
been turned into a Red Cross Hospital, I was brought up to the Ward
where Commandant Connolly had been carried. He was in bed, and I
waited beside him while his wounds were being dressed.   I told
him my orders and asked him did he feel well enough to comply.

Canteen containing two large

onions , part of equipment

worn by Commandant Pearse

when he surrendered at

Moore Street 29 April 1916

Pearse's canteen, containing two large onions.

He said he was, and he read the manifesto which was signed by his Commander-in-Chief.   Commandant Connolly then dictated the following, as he was unable to write himself, which I wrote down underneath Commandant Pearse's typed manifesto and it was signed, and dated April 29/16 by Commandant Connolly:

"I agree to these conditions for the men only "under my own Command in the Moore Street District, "and for the men in Stephen's Green Command."

This document containing the orders of Commandant Pearse and Commandant Connolly was presented on the following day by me to Commandant Thomas MacDonagh who added the following words and signed and dated it 30.IV.1916 3.15.p.m.:

"After consultation with Commandant Ceannt I "have confirmed this Order agreeing to unconditional "surrender."

I shall deal with this later on.

Previous to the surrender of Commandant Pearse I was with the General at the top of Moore Street which was barricaded with sandbags, behind which the British were firing and were being fired at by the rebel forces.   There was the body of an Irish soldier lying in Moore Street and I was informed that it was The O'Rahilly who had been shot shortly before.

The document referred to above in my own handwriting ordering the surrender of their Commands by P.H.Pearse, Commander-in-Chief, James Connolly, Commandant General Dublin Division, and Thomas MacDonagh, Commandant, has been reproduced in facsimile in several publications.

On the night of the 29th April, General Lowe accompanied by myself and two other members of his staff paraded at the Parnell Monument to receive the surrender of the rebels in accordance with their Commander's instructions which had been communicated to their respective Commands in the meantime, and up to 10.30 p.m. about 450 surrendered there.   Of these I took

After the surrender of the GPO garrison, H. E. de C.-W. was ordered to take the prisoners' names. This is the record from the early pages of his Field Message Book of 84 of those names. Among them are: panel 1—John Lemass 2 Capel Street (the future Taoiseach evidently announced himself as Seán, for Harry began his first name as 'Ch' . . . before reverting to English), John Francis McEntee of Belfast (later Seán McEntee, Minister for Finance); panel 3—Harry Boland, 15 Marino Crescent, Lieut. John Plunkett, Larkfield, Kimmage; panel 4—Wm Pearse, St Enda's College Rathfarnham, Michael Collins, 16 Rathdown Road, North Circular Road. Most of the prisoners gave Dublin addresses, but there are names also from Glasgow, Co. Down, Dundalk, Wexford, Tullamore and London. H. E. de C.-W. delegated other officers to complete the total list of 450 men, some from the other Commands.

down the names and addresses of 84 and delegated other Officers
to take the remainder.   The prisoners were drawn up in line
and I walked down the ranks taking down each name and address
as given to me.   As it was physically impossible for me to write
down all the names I sent word to the General that I required
assistance and he then detailed fourteen other Officers to help
me.   The lists made by these Officers were handed in to the
Assistant Inspector General of the Royal Irish Constabulary at a
later date.

I received many expressions of kindliness and thanks
from my rebel countrymen with whom I came in contact and to whom
I was opposed.   Some of those whose names and addresses I took
down personally on that night have held, and now hold, the highest
positions in the Service of the State, which they fought to found, and
others have passed away.   I have reproduced in facsimile the
pages of my note book on which I wrote down by their own direction
those names and addresses.   They were then marched into the en-
closure in front of the Rotunda Hospital.

That night I received orders from the General to be
at the Bank at the corner of Rutland Square and Upper Sackville
Street at 8 p.m. the following morning, Sunday, 30th April, 1916,
to meet the Sinn Fein Nurse, as she was then known to us, and
afterwards as Nurse Elizabeth O'Farrell, who had undertaken to
conduct me to the Headquarters of the various Commands in and a-
round the city for the purpose of communicating the orders to
surrender detailed above.   A military motor car was in waiting,
driven by one of the Royal Army Service Corps motor drivers, with
the Sergeant Major of the 5th Royal Irish Regiment as escort.   I
was unarmed, but Nurse O'Farrell carried an old white apron on a
stick as a flag of truce, and she and I sat behind.

I decided to go to the College of Surgeons, Stephen's
Green, first, which was strongly held by the rebels and which was
keeping up a continuous fusilade with the British garrison

her through the castle up sheps
street to St. Patrick's Park being
the nearest point that the motor
could go to Jacob's Factory as
this and the surrounding neighbourhood
was very strongly held by the rebels.
I was to meet her at 12 noon,
and went to Adjt. H Longridge
Trinity College to have a
party of 25 men & 1 officer
in readiness to take over the
College of Surgeons, when surrendered
It was reported true
by H Carison Adjutant of H
Castle that at 12 noon that
the O.C. troops Shelbourne

69

in the United Service Club and the Shelbourne Hotel. On the
way I had by the General's instructions ordered an escort of
military to be in readiness at Trinity College to take over
the College of Surgeons if the rebels surrendered. At Lambert
Brien's Shop in Grafton Street my motor was brought to a stand-
still owing to the cross firing, and I decided to allow the
Nurse to proceed alone and deliver the document at the College
under cover of the white flag, as both she and it would be
recognised and respected. She returned about 9.30 having delivered the message. Thence I endeavoured to drive her to
Boland's Bakery, Ringsend, but owing to the barricades across
Lower Mount Street, and having tried all the routes down by the
river which were held by the rebels, and reports of continuous
firing further on, I had again to allow the Nurse to proceed on
foot to deliver the document under cover of the white flag.
When she returned unsuccessful at about 11.30 I took her up a-
gain and drove her through the Castle up Ship Street to St.
Patrick's Park, being the nearest point that the motor could
approach to Jacob's Factory as this and the surrounding neighbourhood was very strongly held by the rebels. I was to meet
her again at 12 noon. It will be noted that these visits were
for the purpose of handing in the orders to surrender to the
various Commandants, not to receive their surrenders. Nurse
O'Farrell was very intimate with the situation of all these
Commandes, and had no difficulty in directing the motor which
was the best route to take and where to go next, so that no time
was lost on that account. While waiting in St. Patrick's Park
for the Nurse to return I went to the Castle and obtained inform-
tion from the Garrison Adjutant that a telephone message had been
received from the O.C. Troops, Shelbourne Hotel that the Republican Flag over the College of Surgeons had been hauled down, and
that troops were required to take over the College and the surrender of the Garrison.

      I motored back at once to Trinity College and order-
ed the

.25   7.M: 474251 .

Repeating Pistol in leather Case handed to me by Countess Markievitz when she surrendered to me at College of Surgeons in 1916 with Commandant Mallin . . She kissed the pistol when handing it to m.   H.E.de C. Wheeler

Repeating pistol in a leather case handed to H. E. de C.-W. by Countess Markievicz.

Military Escort which was in waiting to proceed up Grafton
Street as far as possible, and to keep the men out of view of
Stephen's Green as there was still sniping from various points.
From there I went to the Kildare Street Entrance of the Shelbourne
Hotel and interviewed the O.C. troops who pointed out the position
from the top window where he had his maxim gun placed. Having
informed him of my plans, and having telephoned to the O.C.troops
United Service Club not to "open fire" as I was about to receive
the surrender of the rebels, I returned to Grafton Street, picked
up the Sergeant Major with the motor and drove to the front door
of the College of Surgeons. I ordered the Sergeant Major to bang
at the door, and having waited for a reasonable time without any
response, a civilian signalled that there was some excitement
going on down York Street. I went there and saw that a white
flag was hanging out of the side door of the College. Two of the
rebel leaders came out, advanced and saluted. The Commandant
stated that he was Michael Mallin and that his companion was
Countess Markievicz, and that he and his followers wished to
surrender. The Countess was dressed in the uniform of an Irish
Volunteer, green breeches, putties, tunic and slouch hat with
feathers and Sam Brown belt, with arms and ammunition. I asked
her would she wish to be driven in my motor under escort to the
Castle, knowing the excitement her appearance would create when
marching through the streets. She said "No, I shall march at the
head of my men as I am second in Command and shall share their fate"
Accordingly I requested her to disarm, which she did, and when handing over her arms she kissed her small revolver reverently. In
addition to this small automatic pistol, Countess Markievicz was
armed with a German Mauser pistol, which she also handed to me.
This latter was retained by General Lowe until leaving the Curragh,
when he presented it to me, and both are reproduced in the photograph in this article. Commandant Mallin was not armed and I requested him to order his followers to lay

fearing a hostile demonstration by the crowd I offered to lend the Countess Markeovitz in the motor but she stated that she preferred to march out with her men and share their fate as she was Second in Command. The strength stated by her of the Command was 109 men 10 girls and the Commandant & herself.

When the Rebels marched out there was a great demonstration by the crowd which surged in from all sides, and as I could not Spare any of the 25 men Escort I sent to the picket for 4 men and 1 officer to hold the College until a strong guard could

88

Accepting the surrender of the Stephen's Green garrison, H. E. de C.-W. evidently feared 'a hostile demonstration by the crowd' so he offered to escort Countess Markeovitz (as he spelled it) by motor, but she 'preferred to march out with her men and share their fate'. There was 'a great demonstration by the crowd, which surged in from all sides' which greatly hindered his activity.

40 | 1916 SURRENDERS

down their arms in the College and march out and form up in
front of the College.   While they were doing so _I sent a
message to the escort in Grafton Street to come up, as there
were no British troops picketing this part of the city and I
had only 25 men in Grafton Street.   I then inspected the rebels
in the College and ascertained that they had disarmed, and inspected the arms in a large room in the upper part of the building, portion of which had been curtained off as a Red Cross
Hospital.   Commandant Mallin and the Countess Markievicz
accompanied me during my inspection.   The whole building was in
an indescribable state of confusi n and destruction, furniture,
books, etc., being piled up as barricades and the large picture
of the late Queen Victoria torn to pieces and destroyed.   Food,
clothes, arms, ammunition, mineral waters, surgical dressings were
mixed up and lying about in all directions.   On my enquiring about
the wounded, the Countess informed me that they had been removed.
There was one prisoner, Mr. Lawrence Kettle, who was handed over
to me, and whome I drove to the Castle and handed over to the
authorities there.   Having carried out the inspection, I ordered
the Commandant to march out his followers, whom he informed me
numbered 109 men, 10 women, The Countess Markievicz and himself.
I 'phoned from the nearest telephone instrument -- the Mineral
Water Direct Supply Co. at Stephen's Green -- to Headquarters to
inform the General of this surrender.

Immense crowds of civilians had in the meantime
assembled in York Street and Stephen's Green, as there were no
troops guarding this portion of the city, and it was with much
difficulty that the Officer commanding the escort which was small
succeeded in getting the rebels away in safety.   Tremendous
cheers greeted the rebels as they surrendered, and the crowds
followed them and continued this down Grafton Street until I
succeeded in getting a cordon across the street which held the
crowds back at the

Whole time immense crowds in the one of the worst parts of the city pressed in other car but did not appear in any way hostile. However although unfeignedly glad that the fighting was over, it was perfectly plain that all their admiration was for the heroes who had surrendered. Thence we drove back to Jacobs Factory. Here there was a long delay owing to Father Augustine having gone into no 15 Peters St. at the rear of the Factory with McDonagh and we were informed that he was receiving final instructions from the rebels before they surrendered. Eventually owing to the Dense Crowds and the Delay as ...

To H. E. de C.-W.'s surprise the crowd was not hostile, but 'although unfeignedly glad that the fighting was over, it was perfectly plain that all their admiration was for the heroes who had surrendered'. The 'Father Augustine' mentioned on line 11 was a Capuchin who was much involved in facilitating the surrenders, especially of the Jacobs' factory garrison. He later attended Pearse, MacBride and others before their executions.

point of the bayonet and allowed the escort and their prisoners through to safety to the Castle.   In the meantime I
had detailed one N.C.O. and four men to take charge of the
College until a stronger guard could be obtained.   The escort and prisoners reached the Castle Yard in safety at 1.45
p.m.

    I then proceeded to my rendezvous with Nurse
O'Farrell at St. Patrick's Park but was informed that she had
not returned from Jacob's Factory although it was 2 o'clock.
She was to conduct me to the South Dublin Union, Marrow bone
Lane, Distillery and the Broadstone district.   In the meantime General Lowe had accepted the offer of two Franciscan
Monks to persuade the Rebels to surrender, and at 3 o'clock
the General arrived with his staff.   Commandant MacDonagh
and the two monks arrived with a white flag.   By order of the
General I then drove to the back of Jacob's Factory, accompanied by his A.D.C. Commandant MacDonagh and the two monks, and
waited outside in the street, one of the monks holding up the
white flag continuously.   We were detained there for a considerable time, sniping going on close by but not into the
street.   Finally the rebels agreed to surrender in St.Patrick's
Park.   Thence the same party drove to the South Dublin Union
where there was also a considerable delay in obtaining an interview with the Commandant who also finally agreed to march his
men to St. Patrick's Park.   From there accompanied as before
I drove to Marrowbone Lane Distillery over which floated the
Green Flag.   Dense crowds surrounded the motor car and we were
warned that irrespective of the white flag and the monk who was
carrying it, anyone wearing khaki would be fired upon.   In spite
of this nothing unpleasant happened.   However, although there
seemed to be great relief in this district that hostilities had
ceased it was perfectly plain that all the admiration was for
those who had surrendered.

    After this I drove back again to Jacob's Factory
Here there was a long delay owing to Father Augustine having gone

Countess Markievicz walking to the ambulance which carried her to her court martial. The photograph was taken by H. E. de C.-W. and was presented to the President in 1949 and is now in the National Museum of Ireland.

into No. 15 Peter's Street at the rere of the Factory with
McDonagh, and I was informed that he was receiving final instructions from the rebels before they surrendered.   Eventually, owing to the dense crowds and delay as I had to go from
there to Boland's Bakery at Ringsend with Nurse O'Farrell to
deliver Pearse's Notice at the Heqdquarters there, I ordered
the motor to go to Ship Street close to St. Patrick's Park and
wait there for the surrender.

An unpleasant incident then occurred.
Commandant MacDonagh shortly afterwards arrived followed by
crowds and accompanied by the Monk with a white flag, and
stated that although his men had laid down their arms in order
 to surrender, the soldiers had opened fire on them, were throw-
ing bombs into the house, and that the military had broken into
the Factory and were killing his men, and that he had seen one
of our soldiers taking up a position in the Factory and was us-
ing his bayonet.   I told MacDonagh that it was impossible,
as there were no troops there, and that if it was an individual
soldier I did not understand why he and his men could not deal
with him.   He replied that if they interfered with the soldier
they were afraid it might be serious for them.   Commandant
MacDonagh was so positive about the occurrence that I reported
it to the G.O.C. 176th Inf.Brigade and brought MacDonagh before
him.   The General stated that there were none of his troops
there, and he instructed me to ascertain at the Castle whether
any troops had been sent independently.   Accompanied by
General Lowe's A.D.C. I went with MacDonagh to the Castle and
brought him before the Colonel in Command, who also stated that
there were no troops at Jacobs.   I then drove MacDonagh back
and he requested some Officers to go and ascertain the fact.   I
took upon myself to advise strongly against this and refused to
allow General Lowe's A.D.C. to go, pointing out to the G.O.C.
176th Inf.Brigade and to the O.C. troops in the Castle that it
was an impossible story got up for some purpose.   Accordingly, I

Countess Markievicz in the ambulance on the way to her court martial. Note the handcuffs.

told MacDonagh to return accompanied by Nurse O'Farrell,
a priest and the monk who was most vigorous in denouncing
the proceeding, and to order his men to surrender, the G.O.C.
and 176th Inf.Brigade and the O.C. Troops in the Castle having pointed out that if there were soldiers firing at the rere
of the Factory it would not prevent his own men from coming
out at the front of the Factory! Shortly afterwards the two
Monks, the Priest and Nurse Elizabeth O'Farrell returned and
stated there had been no foundation for the accusation against
the military, that none of the Commands had been injured,and
that it was looters ha broken into Jacob's and were doing mis-
chief. I immediately reported this to the G.O.C. 176th Brigade
and to the O.C.Troops at the Castle, and asked them to hear the
Priest on the subject, which they did. Shortly afterwards the
Commander from Marrowbone Lane and from the South Dublin Union
arrived and laid down their arms in St. Patrick's Park along
with the Commander from Jacob's. I then set off again with
Nurse Elizabeth O'Farrell to drive her to Boland's Factory at
Ringsend, but as it was now getting dark and she said she would
prefer to go in the morning I drove to Trinity College with her
and telephoned to General Lowe for instructions. He replied
that the following morning would do, and that in any case it was
reported that the Ringsend Commands had surrendered to the O.C.
Troops, Ballsbridge, and to place Nurse Elizabeth O'Farrell in
the Red Cross Hospital at the Castle until the following morning
leaving her in care of the Matron and not as a prisoner.

        It was on account of this previous surrender
that I did not come in contact with Commandant de Valera who
was in command at Boland's Mill, but I have since met him annually under the most friendly conditions.

        On the night of the 30th April I was invited by
Capt.Purcell to accompany him in his high dog cart to visit the
scenes of the fires which were raging especially in Upper and
Lower

Mauser Pistol handed to me by Countess Markievicz when she surrendered to me at the College of Surgeons Dublin in 1916 with commandant Mallin.

H de C Whelan

This was presented to me by General Lowe

Countess Markievicz's revolver (Mauser automatic pistol) presented to the President and now on display in the National Museum 1916 Exhibition. It is doubtlessly the revolver she used to shoot dead the unarmed police constable Michael Lahiff from Co. Clare as he went about his duties in St Stephen's Green. It has a detachable butt enabling it to be turned into a rifle. It was also referred to as 'Peter the Painter' after an anarchist terrorist who used one in turn-of-the-century London.

Sackville Streets and the adjoining thoroughfares. This was
the first time, owing to the surrender of the Rebels, and the
cessation of hostilities that it was possible for the Fire Brigade
to get down to work and try to combat the fires.

The only other commando was that at Broadstone and the
following copy of Headquarter's Order was delivered to me during
the day in reference to its surrender which owing to the events
which I have narrated it was impossible for me to accept "To/O.C.
4 Dublin Fusiliers, Broadstone, 30.4.16. Captain Wheeler will
arrive in due course to accept surrenders from Rebels. If he
does not turn up, you will accept surrenders taking names and
addresses. Sgd. Staff Officer to G.O.C. Troops Dublin H.O. By
Orderly 11.20 a.m." When I did arrive the Order has been carried
out as directed. After leaving Nurse Elizabeth O'Farrell at the
Castle Hospital I returned to Head Quarters and the following
morning 1st May 1916 was kept busy in Room 13 with various matters
pending the handing over of the Command of the Troops Dublin by
General Lowe to General Sandback which was to take place at 12 noon
General Lowe introduced me to Captain Prince Alexander of Battenberg,
A.D.C. to General Sir John Maxwell, and I accompanied them to the
Inspection held in Trinity College Park of the Irish Regiments
engaged in Dublin during the Rebellion. To each of the Units
General Sir John Maxwell made a speech complimenting them on their
behaviour and praising them for their skill and courage in the
execution of the most distasteful form of warfare to a soldier --
against their own countrymen and house to house fighting. After
luncheon in the College I motored back to Headquarters and from
there I went to deliver a letter from General Lowe to Nurse
Elizabeth O'Farrell and order her release from the Dublin Castle
Hospital.

When I arrived Nurse O'Farrell has been removed from
there to Ship Street Barrack Guard Room by Capt. Stanley, R.A.M.C.
where she was handed over by the O.C. Troops to the Military Police

9065

Small automatic Pistol
(Harrington & Richardson Arms Co
Cal. 25 taken from the arms
in College of Surgeons when it
was surrendered home in 1916

H.G.[ ]Charles

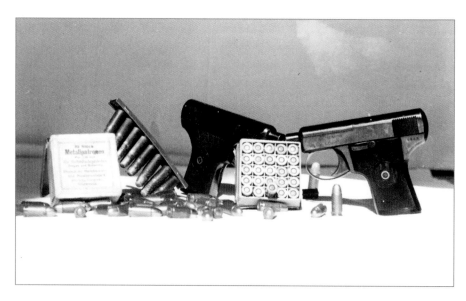

Small automatic pistols recovered from the College of Surgeons after the surrender.

as a prisoner.   Captain Stanley, R.A.M.C. had not been
informed by the Assistant Matron that Nurse O'Farrell was
not to be considered a prisoner, but only to be detained in
the Hospital until sent for by the G.O.C.   Troops Dublin on
this date, and he had therefore discharged her as an ordinary
prisoner when finding her fit.   I considered this a very serious
matter and a grave reflection on the honour of everyone concerned.
I then went to the Provost Marshall and explained the position to
him but he stated that he had sent her to Richmond Barracks, and
that he could give no assistance.   I was determined to have the
matter put right, and it was quite plain that the General would
put all the blame upon me, and in the meantime I was considering
what Nurse O'Farrell must be enduring, and thinking of the grave
breach of faith on the part of the General and his Staff.   Captain
Stanley then procured an Ambulance, and with the Assistant Matron
we went to Richmond Barracks.   I had to await the arrival of
Captain Stanley for over an hour, as he was away on Ambulance
work and I could not act without him.   To my alarm when we
arrived I was informed that Nurse O'Farrell had been sent from
there to Kilmainham.   Every minute was then of consequence as the
prisoners were to be embarked that night for England, and Orders
had been issued for a draft of 400 men to escort the prisoners to
the North Wall, and a detachment of 80 men to form an Over-seas
escort.   At last in great anxiety which was shared by Captain
Stanley and the Assistant Matron we arrived at Kilmainham where I
peremptorily demanded the release of Nurse O'Farrell, and threat-
ened Court Martial if the Orders of the General Officer Commanding
were not complied with forthwith.   This had become necessary as
the Officer Commanding at Kilmainham had already received Orders
from the Provost Marshall that Nurse Elizabeth O'Farrell was to be
deported,

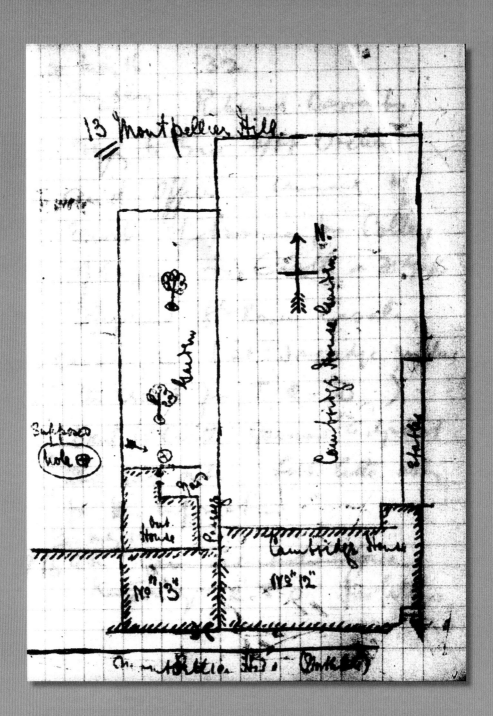

The Field Message Book was criss-cross lined to facilitate map drawing. On this page H. E. de C.-W. identifies for military intelligence a suspected cache of weapons in No. 13 Montpelier Hill, a few doors down from the Royal (since 1922 Collins) Barracks.

and I had no written Order to the contrary, only what I knew
were the General's intentions with regard to her.   I said
I could not leave without Nurse O'Farrell and that I would
send for the General if there was any further delay.

The Assistant Matron and Captain Stanley explained also that it was through a mistake that she had been
allowed to be removed from the Castle and that they were to
blame.

The Officer in charge then handed her over to
me, and she was brought back to the Castle Hospital in the
Ambulance with Captain Stanley and the Assistant Matron, where
we arrived at 5.5. p.m. and I left her there with instructions
as before, that she was to be detained as a patient and not as
a prisoner, until the General issued further Orders.

In the meantime whether by telephone from my-
self or otherwise, General Lowe had heard of the grave mistake
which had been made, and himself chased round in my tracks
until he found her safe in the Hospital where I had left her a
short time before.   He told me that he was not at Headquarters
when my telephone message arrived, but that when he heard of the
position he went round in pursuit himself, and that he had seen
Nurse O'Farrell and ordered her immediate release from the
Hospital.   He then asked me "Why could you not have done that?"
My reply was, as I think it was a bit hard, -- "I had done it
all before you"!   The General and myself were fast friends and
he always said he liked soldiering with me.   It was on account
of the General releasing Nurse O'Farrell that his letter was not
delivered to her, as I never saw her again, and he said it was
unnecessary.   There is a facsimile of this letter produced in
these pages.

The Rebellion was now over.   Of course I was
in the thick of all the other happenings but, as will be
gathered from what I have recorded, I had not time to give

any but superficial attention to what was going on all
round me except my own special Orders which followed and
jostled each other in quick succession. My next duties
were in reference to the Court Martial, as having been present at all the surrenders it was considered that my evidence would be indispensable, the most of my work being to
get intouch with the Officers who were concerned in taking
down the names of those who had surrendered, and tracing
their whereabouts as their Units were all dispersed over
the country. These Courts Martials were held in Richmond
Barracks, (now Griffith's Barracks,) and I was backwards
and forwards continuously during which Mr. Asquith the
Prime Minister crossed from England, paid a visit there and
recommended that the prisoners should be supplied with pil-
lows which were evidently not available (as they were not
a barrack room issue,) for the unexpected addition to the
numbers normally in occupation of those Barrack Rooms!

Martial Law had been proclaimed over the
whole of Ireland and an Order was issued prohibiting anyone
leaving their houses between 7.30 p.m. and 5.30 a.m., and
Licensed premises were only allowed to remain open between
2 and 5 p.m. in the City and County of Dublin, so that the
streets were absolutely empty and deserted. There was no
traffic of any kind, and I seemed to be the only individual
abroad after 7.30 p.m. Being detached from my own Unit I
lived at one of the Hotels, the Shelbourne, or Hibernian,
and after dismissing my official car for the night used to
tramp the streets alone being challenged here and there by
a Sentry. There wasnot a sound, nothing stirring, no lights
visible, and the streets took on quite a different shape and
appearance, and the whole surroundings were weird. My duties
kept me on the go until late at night, amd my notes give the
details of my visits to Richmond Barracks, the Castle, Headquarters Arbour Hill, Kilmainham, Trinity College and elsewhere, interviewing the Officers concerned in the surrenders,
and conferring with the Headquarters Staff in connection with

Martial, and the hour I returned to the Hotel at which I
happened to be staying at the time.

        There were no regular hours for duty during
the time, and we carried on as long as possible each day to
get the work through.

        This went on from the 2nd May until the 16th
May, when I returned to the Curragh.

Irish Independent

IRELAND'S NATIONAL NEWSPAPER.

VOL. 58. No. 102. (INCORPORATING THE "FREEMAN'S JOURNAL"). DUBLIN, SATURDAY, APRIL 30, 1949. PRICE, 1½d.

President Receives
Relics Of Rising

The Irish Times

PRICE 2d.   DUBLIN, SATURDAY, APRIL 30, 1949   No. 28,623

Major de Courcey Wheeler presenting to the President the revolver surrendered to him in 1916 by Commandant General Pearse. Also in the photograph are Mr. Norton, Tánaiste and Minister for Social Welfare, and Colonel O'Sullivan.

Newspaper coverage of H. E. de C.-W.'s handing over of various items to the then President Seán T. O'Kelly (who was part of the GPO garrison in 1916). The Irish Times caption reads: 'Major de Courcy-Wheeler presenting to the President the revolver surrendered to him in 1916 by Commandant General Pearse. Also in the photograph are Mr Norton, Tánaiste and Minister for Social Welfare, and Colonel O'Sullivan.'

The first Court Martial for which my evidence was required was
of P.H.Pearse, Commander-in-Chief at whose surrender to
General Lowe I was present as already recounted, and at 3.45
p.m. on 2nd May 1916 I was detained at Richmond Barracks to give
evidence of identification, and was in consultation with the
Deputy Adjutant General, the Judge Advocate and the Prosecutor
as to procedure.   The evidence in this case was purely formal
on my part, as it was to General Lowe that Commandant Pearse
surrendered unconditionally.   On the 4th May at 9.45 a.m. I was
summoned to Richmond Barracks to give evidence before the Field
General Courts Martial in front of Countess Markievicz of the
surrender of the Rebels at the College of Surgeons.   My state-
ment to the Court as to the surrender of the Rebels was, as I
have already related, and that I asked her would she prefer to
be driven in my car rather than walk through the streets.   She
said "No, I shall march at the head of my men, as I am second
in command, and shall share their fate."   Countess Markievicz
was then asked by the President of the Court whether she wished
to ask me any questions.   She said "No, this Officer has spoken
the truth.   I have no witnesses, what I did was for the free-
dom of Ireland and I thought we had a fighting chance."   I was
then dismissed by the Court.   This was at 12.30. p.m.

Before her marriage Countess Markievicz was
Constance Gore-Booth, eldest daughter of Sir Henry William Gore-
Booth, 5th Baronet, and sister of the present Baronet Sir Joselyn
Gore-Booth of Lissadell, Co.Sligo.   She was a relation of my
wife, (nee Knox), both being descended from Sir Paul Gore, 1st
Baronet of Manor Gore, and to commemorate the event my youngest
daughter who was born on the Curragh a short time before the
Rebellion, was christened Kathleen Constance *constanka* Gore after Countess
Markievicz.   As Miss Constance Gore-Booth I had met her previous-
ly at Castle and other social functions.

On the same day I was again ordered to be present
to give evidence before another Field General Court Martial of the

H. E. de C.-W. with the walking-stick given to him by Commandant Mallin when he surrendered outside the College of Surgeons. This photograph was taken for him with his camera by one of his fellow officers. Sadly, the walking-stick went missing some years later.

surrender of Commandant Michael Mallin who was in command at
the Collect of Surgeons.   My evidence was as described previously: "Commandant Mallin came out of the side door of the College,
advanced and saluted and stated that he was in Command, and that
he and his Command wished to surrender."   The President then
asked Commandant Mallin whether he wished to ask me any questions.
He said "No, but" (turning to me) "I would wish it placed on
record how grateful my comrades and myself are for the kindness
and consideration which Captain Wheeler has shown to us during
this time."   The President of the Court said that his wish would
be carried out; I was then dismissed by the Court.

            In the reproduction of the photograph taken by one
of my brother officers of myself standing by the Ambulance, it
will be noticed that I am carrying a walking stick.   This was
given to me by Commandant Mallin, and was carried by him when he
surrendered at the College of Surgeons.   The Ambulance is that
in which Countess Markievicz was brought to and from herCourt
Martial, and was supplied to the military by the Royal Irish Automobile Club -- the name of which is quite distinct.   In the other
two pictures Countess Markievicz is seen in one, seated in the
Ambulance, and in the other, walking towards the Ambulance after
her Court Martial.

            On the 9th May 1916 I was summoned from Richmond
Barracks to give evidence in Commandant Connolly's case before
a Field General Court Martial which was held in a ward of the
Castle Hospital in which he was a patient and a prisoner.   The
only evidence which I could give was of my interview with him, which
I have previously recorded, when I read Commandant Pearse's
manifesto to him and he dictated his own order which he signed
after I had written it down.   This was produced, and I have included a facsimile reproduction of a duplicate of that document.
The portion in my own handwriting was a copy of that signed by
Commandant Connolly, and the upper and lower parts

H. E. de C.-W. making his speech in connection with the presentation of the 1916 artefacts to President Seán T. O'Kelly. Newspaper coverage of the presentation was extensive. The main daily papers covered it on the front pages and H. E. de C.-W.'s speech was printed in full. It was also broadcast on RTÉ on the 6.30 pm and 10.30 pm news bulletins read by the long-serving newscaster P. P. O'Reilly. The caption to the Irish Times photograph reads: 'The Major concluded his speech by mentioning the appropriateness of the President as the recipient of the mementoes of 1916, because Major Wheeler was Staff Captain to the British Commander and the President himself was Staff Captain to the Irish Commander, Pádraig Pearse.'

are duplicates and bear the original signature of Commandant General Pearse, and the original writing and signature of Commandant MacDonagh.

I now come to the last case in which I was called to give evidence before a Field General Court Martial. This was Thomas MacDonagh, Commandant of the Forces in the District of which Jacob's Factory was the Headquarters, and is one of the Commandos of which I had taken the surrender and of which I have already given an account. On the 7th May 1916, I went with the Deputy Judge Advocate to Mountjoy Prison to examine a ledger entitled "Receipts and Disposal of Prisoners, Private Cash and Property" at page 405, and a motor car was ordered to be at the Prison for the Warder and above ledger, at 10 o'clock the following morning. In the meantime I was ordered to interview the Officer Commanding Amiens Street Station where I arrived at 6 p.m. and was given an Order to enter Liberty Hall. The Printer's type of the proclamation signed by the leaders of the Rebellion was locked in a frame and I took an impression by inking the type and pressing a sheet of paper on it. At 7.15 p.m. a Summary of Evidence was made at Richmond Barracks, and at 7.45 I went to Headquarters. I left there for the Shelbourne Hotel where I was staying, and returned the white Flag which had been made and lent by the Manager when I went to take the surrender of the College of Surgeons. The Hotel placed an historic value on this flag on that account. At 9.45 on the following morning 8th May I arrived at Mountjoy Prison and brought the Warder and Prison ledger as evidence of Commandant MacDonagh's signature. At 10.30 a.m. a Summary of Evidence was taken and I produced the proof of the Proclamation taken by myself at Liberty Hall the night before. At 5.30 p.m. I was again ordered to investigate everything in Liberty Hall, and at 11.15 on the 9th May 1916 I was examined before a Field General Court Martial in Commandant MacDonagh's case. There was a great amount of other evidence, military

Senator Margaret Pearse, on the right of the picture, sister of the executed leader
Patrick Pearse, inspecting the revolvers presented in 1949
(Photo copyright: The Irish Times)

and otherwise. In looking over these notes there does not appear to have been any further evidence necessary in Commandant MacDonagh's case than was given in the other cases in which the surrender in command seems to have been sufficient.

While in Liberty Hall it occurred to me that I would like to have a souvenir of this celebrated building which had been shelled from a gunboat in the river, and as none of the work which I was doing appealed very much to me or appeared attractive I looked out for something more substantial and which perhaps might interest my wife and family. I saw amongst other things a number of sewing machines and as I thought these must have been used in connection with the Rebels' Kit and possibly even by Countess Markievicz, I asked the Officer in charge to save one of them for me. The Officer in Charge immediately complied with my request and said he would have the sewing machine sent to me. Here is the correspondence which passed on the subject:

"To Sergeant,
    Detective i/c.Liberty Hall.

"Motor sent in case you require it. Please let
"me know what arrangements you have made and what
"address will find you. H.E.de C.Wheeler, Capt.
"4 p.m. 10/May/16."

on the back of this document was written this reply:

"Detective Depart.
    Brunswick St.

"Machine just placed on Lorry, sending to Automobile
"Club.   P. Smyth
Capt.Wheeler.

One of the sewing machines used in Liberty Hall for making the green Sinn Féin uniforms.
Having been 'liberated', it gave many years of good service in the Wheeler household.

Probably a few of my readers may be curious
to know some particulars about myself having given so many
about others, so I am doing so as briefly as is consistent
with the actual bearing on the subject of what has gone before.

When England delcared War on Germany on the 4th August
1914 I was on the Reserve of Officers of my regiment the King's
Royal Rifle Corps.   I had been asked by the Major General i/c
of Administration Irish Command, would I take duty with the Army
Service Corps on the Curragh in the event of mobilization.   I
said Yes, and went through a voluntary course of instruction with
this brance of the Service.

On the declaration of War I joined up and took over
command of the Army Service Corps in the Curragh District, which
included Newbridge, Kildare, Naas, Maryborough, Birr and Coolmoney at Glen Imaal.

Having seen all the units of the 5th Division depart
I had to recommend Officers from the Reserve for Appointment
to fill the places of the Officers of the Army Service Corps who
had left to carry on the duties required by the Units which were
been newly formed.   I was engaged in the organisation of this
work when I received a telegram on the 10th August from the War
Office only one week after taking over my command, to join forthwith my Battalion of the King's Royal Rifle Corps at Winchester
in England.   I knew that this was an error owing to the over-
lapping of Administrative and Personell departments but I had to
comply, and again having handed over my command I hurried to
Robertstown to say good bye to my wife and children.   Herea
very interesting event took place.   When I arrived at the villag
the Irish National Volunteers were lined up on each side of the
street, and Mr. James Dowling in Command, read an address as follows:--

"Robertstown, 10 Aug.1914.
Col. H.E.De Courcy Wheeler.

"We the members of the Robertstown Company of Irish
National Volunteers beg to offer to Col.H.E. de Courcy Wheeler

Lt. General Sir Brian Mahon, commanding 10th Division, leaving the Curragh railway siding.
The photograph was taken by H. E. de C.-W.

our regret that he has been called away from his young wife
and family to fight the cause of his country in Belgium.   At
same time we congratulate him on the fact that the Government
has selected him and promoted him to rank Colonel --- to take
his place in such a sacred cause.

We wish him to convey to his Regiment that the
cause for which they are about to fight has the entire sym-
pathy of the Irish National Volunteers and for which they are
also willing to take up arms (if they had them) if necessary
and required.

We assure Colonel Wheeler that Mrs. Wheeler and
his family, and property will be safe in the hands of the Irish
Volunteers until he returns.

Wishing Colonel Wheeler God speed and success.

On behalf of Volunteers,

James Dowling Commdg."

The whole village had turned out to shake hands with me and I
made a short speech in reply thanking them, and hastned away to
report at Headquarters and embark for England.

Somewhere between Dublin and Kingstown I received
a telegram that a motor despatch rider was in pursuit of me
with a telegram from the War Office ordering me to return to the
Curragh.   Telegrams had been sent by my friends on the Curragh,
and also from Robertstown, where the despatch rider had first
been sent, but was just too late, to stop me.   This, of course,
created a great deal of pleasurable excitement all through the
countryside, but all I knew of it was that I was off to the Front.

On my return to the Curragh where the Command was
again handed back to me I sent the following reply to the fare -
well address of the Irish National Volunteers:

"Curragh Camp,
10 August 1914.

"Dear Sir,

Upon reaching Dublin en route for Winchester today
"my journey was interrupted by a telegram from the War Office
"directing me to remain at the Curragh.   My arrangements had

"accordingly at once to be changed and I returned to camp
"that evening.

"   The kind and interesting ceremony at Robertstown
"when the Irish national Volunteers turned out, and I was
"presented with an address has thus been rendered so far a
"its main purpose was concerned, unavailing.   But I write
"to say that for me and mine it is not and never will be un-
"availing, for we shall never forget the goodness of heart,
"the neighbourliness and the real friendship which prompted
"the demonstration.   And I ask you to permit me to retain the
"Address as a memento of the goodwill of all those friends on
"whose behalf it was drawn up and presented.   I hope to prove
"worthy of such kindness in the future.

"   There is one passage in your Address to which I must
"especially refer.   It has touched me deeply, and it is with
"absolute confidence that I leave, when called upon to do so,
"my wife and my children and my property in the safe custody of
"the Robertstown Company of the Irish National Volunteers. As a
"small token of my great gratitude to them, I enclose a donation
"to your funds which I hope will help to carry out the objects
"we all in this crisis have so much at heart.

                        I remain, dear Sir,
                             Very faithfully yours,
                        Henry E.de Courcy-Wheeler,
                                   Capt.

"To/ Mr. James Dowling,
    (late Royal Irish Constabulary)
        Commdg.Robertstown Company, Irish National Volunteers,
            Robertstown, Co.Kildare."

On the next day the 11th August 1914 I received the following
delightful and valued letter:

                        "Robertstown,
                         11 August 1914.

"Dear Sir,

"   I beg to regret my absence from Robertstown yesterday
"which prevented me from being in the Market Square to join in
"seeing you away -- but you were scarcely gone until there was
"general rejoicing in the village at the good news of your return

"among us again and I humbly hope for a long time, for indeed
"my feelings were deeply touched when I saw you waving your
"handkerchief to your good lady.
"   With every good wish.
                              I beg to remain, dear Sir,
                                Yours faithfully,
                                  Jas. Sullivan."
Capt. H. de C. Wheeler.

          Shortly after this I transferred my wife and family
to the Commanding Officers' Quarters on the Curragh where they
lived until I was demobilized, and on the 11th September 1914
my twin daughters were born there.   In the meantime the battle
for Nancy which began on the 26th August was raging between the
French and Germans who had attacked the country with overwhelming
forces to the East and North of that city, and on the 11th
September 1914 the French after 19 days desperate fighting recovered the whole of the ground and saved Nancy, and put the
Germans in full retreat.

          To commemorate this great Victory by the French one of
the twins was christened Nancy, and the other Joan after the
Maid of Orleans, who had not then been canonized.   Being French
also on their mother's side, descended from the Count de Ligondes
of Auvergne, General in the French Army, whose grand-daughter
married the Right Honourable John Beresford, it seemed peculiarly
appropriate that those happy events should have taken place just
at the same time.

          With my three children, Wigstrom, Dorothea and Annesley,
whom I brought from Robertstown and my three daughters born on the
Curragh I had now six living in my Quarters when the Rebellion
broke out, and this naturally caused anxiety when I was ordered
away on duty elsewhere.   One very amusing incident occurred.
There was electric light in my Quarters the back of which over-
looked the Curragh towards the Race Course Stand House and
Newbridge.   I had a large household of eleven when I was away,
not counting my Groom and Gardener.   It can easily be understood

that the switching on and off of the electric light was fairly
frequent and rapid during the children's bed hour and getting
ready for dinner.   It was reported to the G.O.C. by the Intelligence
Department that Morse Code signals had been located in my house
signalling to the Rebels who were supposed to be creeping up the
slope to attack and seize the Camp during the absence of the troops
who had been ordered away to put down the Rebellion.   The
Intelligence Officer was very determined and persistent about it --
and I for once got angry, and brought him before the General, and
pointed out that he had made himself very ridiculous, as my quarters
there were open to inspection, and there were only women and children
in the house, and that all the Officers of the Headquarters Staff
knew that I was actually engaged in receiving the surrender of the
rebels at the time.

My duties while stationed on the Curragh extended to
Newbridge, Kildare, Naas, Maryborough, Birr and Coolmoney Barracks
at Glen Imaal.   I was responsible for the accommodation of
troops at these Barracks at all these Stations, and for the
equipment of the Barracks in every detail, the Officer Commanding
Royal Engineers being responsible for the condition of the
building and this brought me in instant contact with the C.R.E.
who became a great friend and we were able to co-operate in
every emergency.

After a time owing to the constant changing of troops
I knew every room in every building in all these places, and
everything that should be in them and everything that wasn't, as
I had to have an inspection at every marching out of a Unit and
at every marching in, to check the damages and the deficiencies
for which the regiment had to pay or was supposed to pay.   That
was where the fun began. The regiment marched off to the Front
and a bill was mounted up against them of sometimes hundreds of
pounds.   There were several of between £400 and £700.   It was
no use trying to get paid by a regiment which was on its way to,
or actually fighting at France, so the amount was promptly

written off.   I had Brigades of various Nationalities to deal
with.   One was a Scottish Brigade, their Barrack damages amounted
to over £400 when they were marching out after a comparatively
short stay on the Curragh.   The debt was written off to all but
a sum of One pound two shillings and sixpence.   The Scotch
Commanding Officer disputed this sixpence and a voluminous correspondence passed between my department and the regiment concerned
-- I even appealed to their sense of humour having been made a
present of hundreds of pounds that it was not much to ask them to
pay 6d which was due -- but they did not see any humour in a
Scotch regiment parting with sixpence!

                Another experience was new to me.   Before I had been
long on the Curragh I was informed that the Official Auditors were
coming down to audit.   So I waited as I had not the remotest idea
what auditing had to do with troops going to the Front; they had
taken away everything with them and left nothing that was any use.
The Auditors came down and I received them in my Office.   I did not
know what they were talking about -- they referred me to the regulations.   That was my chance, just at the psychological moment I
took the waste paper basket from under the table -- I had put the
King's regulations and the Barrack Regulations and all supplemen-
tary Regulations into it.   "Look here", I said "there are the regulations and if I had known anything about them or used them not a
single Unit would have been able to leave the Curragh!"   The
Auditors were secretly delighted but intimated that I must have had
great influence at my back to keep me there.   I knew nothing about
that but later understood why.   Whenever I was ordered away the
invariable reply to War Office was "indispensable at the Curragh"!
From my arrival at the Curragh I messed with the 10th Reserve Regiment of Cavalry and I had a very happy time with them.   The Commanding Officer became my great friend.   It was the usual custom in
those days for the Cavalry Officers to have refreshment in the shape
of a glass of Port in the Mess "after stables" that is after their
morning.————

inspection of their Chargers, saddlery etc. I had not to
attend their laborious parade, but I joined them in the refreshment which was very agreeable and necessary before attending to next duties.

I didn't know for a long time why my brother
Officers in this Mess were so anxious that I should join them
in a game of "Snooker" after luncheon or after Mess at certain
times. I found when my Mess bill came in that they had been
short of pocket money!

The Cavalry had a great contempt for the Infantry.
At times it was necessary when the accommodation at the Curragh
was over-flowing to mix up the Units. On one occasion the
Officer commanding a Cavalry Regiment was most indignant with
me for having accommodated some of his men in an Infantry Barracks
-- "because they would be contaminated!" But everything at
all times wasnot a matter of course. I had prodigious hard
work. Mine was an administrative job and required an immense
amount of organisation to cope with the movements of troops, and
I had an immediate staff of seventy-three; and as the work was
new on mobilization I had to see that there were no mistakes made.
Naturally then on more than one occasion "I was" -- as they say
in the Army -- "for it"! Then another on one occasion came to
my Quarters late at night -- this particular Officer was a great
friend -- "You've put me in the cart, I'm ruined!!" Anyhow I
got him out of the cart, and on the other occasions I wiped my
feet and didn't get it in the neck. But there was a dispute
over my position between the Major-General i/c Administration and
the General Officer Commanding the Troops. I was actually under
orders to the former and therefore should not have complied with
the orders of the G.O.C. troops without

the former's permission.   When the Rebellion broke out I was
Officer i/c Barracks on the Curragh, and in the first instance
subject to discipline under the Officer Commanding the Army
Service Corps.   But I had made this an independent command,
-- had become "O.C. Barracks" and was known to my friends as
"Barracks."   Every day I was in direct communication by telephone or Orderlies with not only the Major-General i/c Administration, but also with the Staff of the Commander-in-Chief;   and
with each successive General Commanding the Troops on the Curragh
I was in constant touch.   Therefore, whe I was ordered to join
General Lowe's Staff at Headquarters Irish Command for the
Curragh during the Rebellion, I had no hesitation in complying
without applying for further leave to do so;   also there were no
troops during that time to accommodate.   But when the actual
Rebellion was over, I was had up before the Major General i/c
Administration represented by the Assistant Director of Supplies
and Transport for being absent without leave of the O.C. A.S.C.
The G.O.C. said he had given me the order, and M.G.A. told him he
had no authority to do so, and the General said he had.   Anyhow,
at the interview I informed the Assistant Director of Supplies
and Transport, that not only had I received orders from the
General Officer Commanding to join his Staff, but that I had actually told the O.C.A.S.C. that the General might call upon me at
any time to go to Dublin, and that he had raised no objection.
It was between 11 and 12 o'clock at night when I got the order,
and it seemed unreasonable to get him up out of bed at that hour
to inform him.   The M.G.A. accepted my explanation, complimented
me on my work and said he was sorry, that there had been a misun-
derstanding, shook hands and told me to report when I had finished
my work in connection with the Rebellion.

Outgoing Units had evidently given their successors the tip
that they could get any information they wanted from "O.C.
Barracks" and accordingly I was consulted on every imaginable
subject. For instance, one of the General's Staff had a "Tin
Lizzie" which he used a lot on military duty, and during a
heavy frost the radiator bust and he could not get it mended
and there was not one to be had for love or money as the War
Office had commandeered all spare parts of Ford Cars. He came
to consult me. He nearly embraced me when I told him I had a
spare radiator which I had secreted at my home and that he could
have it if he would replace it. He promised to do so and
carried out his promise, and told everyone that I could supply
anything from a radiator to a married quarter!

The demand for married quarters by married Officers
was never ceasing. As one regiment marched out, another marched
in, and the accommodation for married and single had to be handed
over to the new arrivals. But this was a delicate question.
Should Officers on Active Service be allowed to bring their
families to a military camp like the Curragh where all the accommodation was required for troops, and where all the married
soldiers' quarters had been vacated for this purpose and their
wives and families sent away? I had to deal with these appli-
cations and take the responsibility, because if conflicting
claims had to be referred to Headquarters I was "for it" for
allowing any married Officers family to occupy them which was
contrary to Orders. However I carried on, and Headquarters did
not intervene. In my own case my quarters were allotted for the
accommodation of so many single Officers, but although there were
many frontal attacks to turn me out, and a Board of Officers was appointed
the whole question of my allotment of the married quarters on the
Curragh, my family remained in possession, and the Board of Officers
Inquiry upheld my decisions in all the other cases.

There was a pressing need for dressings for the wounded Over-seas and at home. Two ladies formed depots at their private residences on the Curragh at which they and their friends, generally Officers' wives, met and devoted all their available time to making bandages and dressings to keep up the supply for the urgent and ever increasing demand. It was found that a certain moss was peculiarly suitable for antiseptic and absorbent dressing of wounds known as "Sphagnum Moss". At one of these Depots -- the Curragh War Hospital Supply Depot -- this Sphagnum Moss was required, and as it was not then well known, nor where it could be found I was asked to conduct a party of these ladies to a bog to point it out and show them how to gather it. In spite of my warnings some of them stepped on the most alluring spring-green patches of this dripping growth and sank over their knees in the treacherous slime before they were rescued -- but it was Summer time ! It is not generally known that the turf which we burn consists altogether of this ninety-three per cent moisture growth compressed after thousands of years of decomposition into liquid mud which is then cut and dried for fuel. Nor could I anticipate that the Rebels who surrendered to me on that 30th April 1916 -- and now Rulers of the State -- would be sitting, after many years had elapsed, as my friends and my honoured guests annually at a festive board on one of these bogs to encourage the production and use of this turf for fuel which in its primitive state made dressings for the wounds which their opposing forces inflicted on each other.

The wounded and those invalided home needed entertainment. I had a drawingroom Pathescope and a Gramophone which were in frequent demand at the Hospital and Headquarters Hut by the General for this purpose. Then there were entertainments in aid of the Red Cross at the Gymnasium and Miss Sandes Soldiers' Home, and I still have the seating plans made by the C.R.E.' Department for a special occasion at which the

Gervais Elwes and Miss Margaret Cooper were the Artistes.

For ourselves, who never knew when we would be ordered to the Front or return from it, we organised such relaxation as we could to make us forget "the fear of being afraid" when that time came -- for panic is nothing compared to the anticipation of it. But there was little opportunity for much in the way of sport.

We always managed "The Glorious Twelfth" and a day at the Partridge, and riding being an essential part of an Officer's training, hunting was a recognized parade at which every Officer not on duty was entitled and expected to attend; and they hunted their Chargers which was also a vexed question got over by the above unwritten law. In my case I had my own hunter, but could not draw forage for it unless it was War Office property. This was got over by selling it to the Government with permission to retain it as a Charger, which worked out very well indeed! There was of course the question -- Was the Officer i/c Barracks entitled to a Charger? -- but it was argued that I had long distances to cover in the course of my duty, and that a horse would save petrol! but in any case that being attached to the Army Service Crops I was entitled to a Charger.

We improvised a four-in-hand which is seen in the photograph at Nas-na-Riog Hotel. There was a long spell of skating, and we had Ski-ing and Tobogganing on the hills over the Rifle Ranges after Mess in the moonlight, and we had Garrison Sports and the Curragh Races, and Hockey Matches - both Ladies and Mixed - with Scratch teams got together by my wife who was an International, and played for Ireland many times; and tennis parties, and dances in the Sports Club, and love affairs, and the inextricable and inexplicable "triangle," and things told in secret, which I cannot ever allude to, and separations and reunions, and welcomes and farewells!!

There was censorship of news from the Front and
fabricated accounts began to come through from "Eyewitness"
attached to General Headquarters, -- irreverently known as
"Eyewash" on the Curragh -- which were promptly rectified
by arrivals of those on leave and invalided home.   Very soon
we found that our successes were really disasters, which we
had not been accustomed to in previous Wars, and one of these
was Mons at the beginning of the War.   We had heard of the
"Angels of Mons" and the marvellous feats performed by our men.
But when survivors began to arrive at the Curragh from the very
scene of Action, and told us of the real state of affairs --
we were disillusioned.   The climax was when one Junior
Officer turned up with an unfamiliar ribbon on his jacket, and
explained that it meant "escaped"!   It was the ribbon of the
"Mons Star" which the Chief Staff Officer of one of the
Generals who had returned from the Front told me he had refused to put up and was then faced with a Court Martial if he
disobeyed the Order.   This Junior Officer had been transferred
to the Royal Flying Corps, and was amongst the first of those
who came over with the 19th Squadron to the Aerdrome on the
Curragh.

The hangars for the Aeroplanes had been erected
just outside my garden fence.   The advent of the first flying
machine nearly made me crazy with enthusiasm.   I was brought
up, and applied to be transferred to the Royal Flying Corps.
The Officer Commanding had me tried with all kinds of stunts
and recommended my application which was approved, but Irish
Command blocked it with the formula which I have mentioned, so
I could not join, for which disappointment the only consolation
I got was "you ought to be devoutly thankful!"   I took a
photograph of a group, including one of the Generals, on the
Aerodrome at the

Curragh standing beside the first Aeroplane belonging to No. 19 Squadron.

Then there was the story round the sinking of the Lustania and why she had not been escorted when it was known before she sailed from New York that she would be torpedoed; that the Lusitania arrived in Liverpool flying the United States Flag; that the United States Government sent a note to the British Government, and that the controversy became keen on 11th February 1915 on the abuse of the Neutral Flag by ships of Belligerents; that the German Government had announced their intention of a submarine blockade of Great Britain, and sank the Lusitania a few miles off the old Head of Kinsale with tremendous loss of life, including American citizens which led to far reaching results; the United States joined the Allies and transported millions of American recruits to France without whom we would have lost the war; and the loss of Sir Hugh Lane, a personal friend, who went down with the ship, carrying with him whatever intentions he had of presenting his priceless collection of modern paintings to Ireland and causing another breach in the friendly relations between the two countries. But we had heard also that on or about the same date, which turned out to be momentous, of the project of closing the Straits of Dover by lines of gigantic steel nets to intercept the submarines, and the arrival of the first "Tanks" and smoke screens at the Front, and this made us realise that in spite of the gloom which seemed to have settled on all of our operations, there were a few active brains working effectively for the safety of the Empire.

Another disturbing account was that of the Naval attack on the Dardanelles in 1915 with no result except in the loss of ships and men, and then new arrivals told of the advantage this was to the Turks because it prepared them for the landing of the troops which was not commenced until six weeks later, and the appalling loss of life through the disagreement of the Divisional Commanders and their refusal to obey their Chief who was hated, and the landing at Suvla Bay in 1915 of reinforcements, including the 10th Division which was raised at the Curragh and all of whom I knew, and all too late, and the final total evacuation of Gallipoli in January 1916; and the disastrous Battle of Jutland in May 1916 which resulted in the tying up of a large portion of our Fleet to watch the German Fleet which has escaped and remained in being, through Admiral Jellicoe's slogan "Safety First" which has since been adopted on the cars of the Dublin United Tramway Company to save themselves ! and the tragic end to Lord Kitchener in June 1916 with the news of which arrived simultaneously the rumour of foul play by those in Power who had ordered him to Russia; and Lord Kitchener's previous inspiration to the Press that Russian Troops had arrived in the South of England through Scotland in shuttered Railway carriages for France to roll up the right wing of the enemy. And one Officer who arrived shortly afterwards on the Curragh told us that he had been stationed close to their encampment, and that he had seen them, and another Officer told me that he had ventured to open one of the doors of the Railway carriages and was convinced because he had actually seen snow in it, and I had no further doubt about the matter ! And then I had information from others of the secret preparations for the Battle of the Somme, and of the intention to explode a dump of ammunition, which would be so terrific that the King could hear it in London, as a signal for the Battle to begin. And we heard at the same time of the shortage of shells. The dump was exploded and it must have been gigantic in mass and noise because it was easily heard in London from the Somme. But owing to the waste of this ammunition the supply of shells was exhausted in a few days, there were no

roads which had to be constructed, there was no water which
had to be laid on in pipes, and the whole ground over which
our troops had to advance was a sea of mud.   The further
story was that the Germans had withdrawn their first line
troops when the signal of the explosion shook the ground,
and replaced them with old men and boys just to keep up the
pretence of resisting, and that the Germans gradually
retired drawing on our men until in October they formed up
on the previously prepared "Hindenburg Line" leaving our
men for their winter quarters in misery in the mud; and
I was told by a Brigade's General who returned from the
Battle that our casualties were over four hundred and ninety
thousand and so on.   All these events were taking place
before, during and immediately after the Easter Rebellion
in 1916, so that my readers will understand what an
important part it actually played in these critical times,
when some of the best of my countrymen were bearing the
brunt of these stupendous battles in foreign lands, and
were not available, and had no knowledge of what was going
on at home.   And, so having retold these tales in the way
they were told to me, it seems that the only thing left
for me to tell about myself, is my age.   I am the same age
as the Non-Commissioned Officer who is seen in the photograph
with me.   We were both born on St. Patrick's Day, in the
same year, and are celebrating the event in the garden of
my quarters on the 17th March 1916!   The garden with its
tennis ground was the best on the Curragh;   both of my
predecessors were gardeners, and had kept it in
perfect order;   but, as anyone who had a garden
on the Curragh knows, it was subject to sudden

raids and was devoured periodically by hungry sheep, which seemed able to scent every new blade the moment it put its nose above the ground.   Even the Goat, which was too old to go to the Front with its Regiment, and left behind with me on their departure, was a Saint in comparison to those Diabolical thieves, and is seen in the photograph quite at home at the Children's Party!   It was said that a Curragh Sheep would die if it stopped eating for five minutes!   But there was no redress for these infuriating acts of trespass, and I knew enough about law not to go to law.   Being a member of the Irish Bar my opinion was often asked on various questions both officially and by my friends, and being a Magistrate my servies, at Petty Sessions on the Curragh and elsewhere, were constantly requisitioned by the Resident Magistrate and the Royal Irish Constabulary, so that I had a varied experience during this time, and this was one of the reasons that General Lowe ordered me to join his Staff in Dublin.

It will be seen that all these incidents which I have related have a direct bearing on how I became involved in the Rising of Easter Week 1916.   The account has not been in any way polished or augmented from any outside source, as will be immediately apparent, because it would have lost its atmosphere of veracity and contempoarary association, back to which I have forced myself after years of separation in thought and deed which had been obliterated by the sorrows and struggles through which all of us have passed since the 4th August 1914.

APPENDIX 1

H. E. de Courcy-Wheeler's daughter, Dorothea, aged 106

We transferred from Robertstown House to the Curragh Camp in 1914 where my father took up his duties as Officer in charge of the services side in the barracks. My father desperately wanted to go and fight in the Great War. He got called up twice and then called back to the Curragh. He wanted action. When an airfield was set up and the first planes arrived at the Curragh, he was crazy with enthusiasm and tried to transfer to the Royal Flying Corps. But his application was refused.

I was only five at the time and I remember being in the back seat with nanny and my baby brother Annesley with a big silver tray on our knees. We were in Daddy's Ford car with canvas roof and windows that we took down if it wasn't windy. The car had big kerosene lamps. It had to be wound up to start, often with a back kick, which nearly broke an arm. Mother and Father were in the front seats and the villagers stood at the gate waving goodbye. The silver tray belonged to the family and was used for tea in the afternoons. The house was locked for the duration of our stay at the Curragh.

We moved to a large square house on the edge of the Curragh plains, with a big garden around it. The air-force was stationed outside our back gate. My father had his horse in the stables and there was a man looking after the house. I think he doubled as groom and houseman. We had a cook, a parlour-maid and a nurse. My twin sisters, Joan and Nancy, were only just two and the youngest, Kathleen, in her cradle.

My mother was an ex-hockey international so she immediately organised a hockey team with the army and officers. The officers' mess was next door to us. They used to play hockey down on the grass at the bottom of the garden and the officers would come back to our house afterwards. [And the hockey sticks?] Oh, we fashioned them out of the hedgerows!

I remember going to church and my mother had a lovely sunshade, which I now have. And I had a parasol to match my mother's parasol, though mine was frilly! There was a Colonel Portal* and he had six children and I used to play with them a lot. There was a lake or pond in his garden in the Curragh and they had a raft that they used to go out on, and I fell in when I was getting on to the raft.

It was terribly cold in the winter on the Curragh and my mother used to stitch my father into newspapers under his tunic, his military jacket, to keep out the biting wind and the cold. I remember very distinctly standing in the study watching the sewing.

I remember going up, with my mother, into the water-tower on the Curragh, which was very high, to look at the flames in Dublin—you could see them from the top of the water-tower. I was seven then.

[This interview was recorded in 1999.]

*Colonel Portal of the 3rd Reserve Cavalry brigade was Commander of the Curragh Mobile Column. He was ordered by General Lowe to establish a cordon around the west side of the city to cut off the rebel leaders from their outposts. It was his idea to make the armoured vehicles with boilers from Guinness' brewery and the railway works.

APPENDIX 2

Harry had no idea that his brother Billy was also in the thick of it during the Easter Rising. Billy, who was born in Dublin in 1879, the fourth of Harry's five brothers, was one of 'the most distinguished surgeons in Ireland at the time'. He was the Irish representative on the War Office Council of Consulting Surgeons. He was mentioned in dispatches for treating wounded soldiers, under fire during the Rising. On Easter Monday, ignoring snipers, he made his way across Saint Stephen's Green to Mercer's Hospital to attend an officer with a chest injury. Two days later he attended a soldier at the corner of Dawson Street in the small hours. He also administered to two officers of the Sherwood Foresters who were wounded in Fitzwilliam Street. On another occasion, in Upper Mount Street, 'an old lady of seventy-three was shot through the leg in her own room, and was taken to Dr W's home, where she had to have her leg amputated'. He was but one of many doctors and nurses who did heroic work attending to the wounded.

In Mercer's Hospital Billy, with two other eminent surgeons and an able nursing staff, treated about 130 citizens, rebels and soldiers suffering from gunshot wounds. This was in addition to those he dealt with in the street and at his own nursing home at 33 Upper Fitzwilliam Street. He had placed this at the disposal of the St John's Ambulance Brigade and the British Red Cross at the beginning of World War I as a hospital for wounded officers. He was also surgeon to the Duke of Connaught's Hospital in Bray for limbless soldiers.

The story was the same in the other Dublin hospitals. Nearer Mount Street Bridge Sir Patrick Dun's was filled to overflowing with wounded. Some 40 bullet wounds of a 'shocking nature' were treated and 12 of these proved fatal. In the Royal City of Dublin Hospital, Baggot Street, upwards of 200 wounded were being treated. An example of the bravery in the medical profession is exemplified by a colleague of Billy's in Mercer's, Dr John Lumsden, the most eminent physician in Dublin at the time. 'The conduct of JL was simply magnificent. He coolly and calmly knelt in the middle of the road attending to wounded soldiers while bullets were flying from houses on both sides.' John Lumsden was knighted in 1918 and Billy in 1919.

In 1939 Billy became consulting surgeon to the Admiralty and was now Surgeon Rear-Admiral Sir William Ireland de Courcy-Wheeler, but of course remained Billy to family, friends, colleagues and citizens in the city he loved. Of it he wrote: 'There have been times in the recent history of this country when some of us tired of the turmoil, bewildered at the outlook, anxious for the safety of our families, felt inclined and were offered temptation to seek peace elsewhere. The impulse was fleeting for in the whole wide world whether in peace or in war there is no place like the city in which we live.'

He died suddenly and unexpectedly in 1943, aged 64, while dressing for a dinner at which he was to be the guest speaker.

Sources: *The Quality of Mercer's: The Story of Mercer's Hospital, 1734–1991* and *An Assembly of Irish Surgeons*, both by J. B. Lyons, in which Billy's medical career is told at length; *Dublin Historical Record* Volume L, No 2, 1997, in which Anthony Kinsella writes a 33 page article on 'Medical Aspects of the 1916 Rising'; and *The Sinn Féin Rebellion as I saw it,* (1991) by Mary Louisa Hamilton Norway who was living in the Royal Hibernian Hotel, Dawson Street, at the time and wrote letters to her sister on the events as they happened. Her husband was Secretary of the General Post Office with his office in the GPO. He added his chapter 'Irish Experiences in War'. She was a friend of Billy and his wife Elsie and describes him as 'Surgeon to the Forces in Ireland'.

See also the chapter on Easter 1916 and on the Wheeler Family in *Findlater's, The Story of a Dublin Merchant Family* (2001), which is on-line www.findlaterbook.com

APPENDIX 3

THE PEARSE SURRENDER PHOTOGRAPH:
WHO IS WHO IN THE PHOTOGRAPH AND WHO TOOK IT?

The photograph opposite shows the famous moment when Patrick Pearse formally surrendered to General Lowe. To clarify those in the picture, the officer beside General Lowe is the General's son, his ADC, Lieutenant John Lowe (who later became a Hollywood actor under the name of John Loder, and was briefly married to Hedy Lamarr). The General and his son belonged to a cavalry regiment, the Reserve Cavalry Brigade, and the ADC is seen in the regiment's military khaki breeches and putties. In contrast, H. E. de C.-W's. uniform is that of an infantry regiment, The King's Royal Rifles, as seen in the photograph taken outside the College of Surgeons on the following day (see page 58). Also the facial features and height are clearly of father and son. H. E. de C.-W. was a slight man of medium build.

The feet of a person behind Pearse are those of the Red Cross nurse, Elizabeth O'Farrell, referred to at the time as the Sinn Féin nurse. On closer inspection, the hem of a woman's skirt and shoes can be seen. In an account published in 1959 in *An Fiolar* (Cistercian College Roscrea annual) Elizabeth O'Farrell is quoted: 'When I saw a British soldier getting ready to take a photo, I stepped back beside Pearse so as not to give the enemy press any satisfaction'.

When the picture was first published in the *Daily Sketch*, London on the 10th May 1916 her feet had been removed from the picture. It is not clear why.

Why is H. E. de C.-W. not seen in the photo? In his account he says: 'At 2.30 pm Commandant General Pearse, Commander-in-Chief, surrendered to General Lowe accompanied by myself and his A.D.C. at the junction of Moore Street and Great Britain Street, and handed over his arms and military equipment. His sword and automatic repeating pistol in holster with pouch of ammunition and his canteen which contained two large onions were handed to me by Commandant General Pearse. His sword was retained by General Lowe.'

How did he take the photo while holding the surrendered items? In the photo it can be seen that General Lowe has what looks like the sword, and, on close perusal, more. So the photo was taken prior to receiving the pistol, pouch, canteen and ammunition.

The Pearse Surrender photograph
Surrender of Commandant Pearse to Brigadier General Lowe, 29th April 1916

Who took the historic photograph of the surrender? Nurse O'Farrell's remark 'When I saw a British soldier getting ready to take a photo' rules out a press photographer. In the Cashman Collection in the RTÉ Archive it is stated: 'According to our documentation, this image is reproduced from a negative taken by an amateur photographer who was a British Army officer at the scene, and who gave the negative to Joseph Cashman".

H. E. de C.-W.'s papers in the National Library include several photographs. He mentions them in his record of the surrenders and cross references them with the text. It is clear from his text that he carried a camera with him (probably a Kodak collapsible which would fit into his uniform pocket). He writes: 'In the reproduction of the photograph taken for me by one of my brother officers standing by the ambulance it will be noticed that I am carrying a walking stick'. About another, of the Singer sewing machine in Liberty Hall, he states: 'when I photographed it' and of another: 'I took a photograph of a group, including one of the Generals, on the Aerodrome at the Curragh'. He must have included the camera in his kit with intent, and he had not much time to pack: 'On the 28th April at 10.30 pm I received an order . . . to report immediately to General Lowe's staff . . . at Park Gate Street. I got my kit ready, borrowed a loaded revolver, overhauled my motor car and left the Curragh alone as the water-tower clock was clanging midnight'.

He was well abreast with then modern technology: In the Curragh Camp: 'The wounded and those invalided needed entertainment. I had a drawing-room Pathescope [early ciné -films] and a Gramophone which was in frequent demand at the Hospital'.

Summary: It can't be proved categorically who took the photograph but there is circumstantial evidence supporting the claim that it was H. E. de C.-W.

APPENDIX 4

THE SURRENDER OF COMMANDANT DE VALERA

In his text H. E. de C.-W. writes about the difficulties in delivering the surrender notes to the various garrisons, owing to the continuing sniping from roof-tops. Clearly a British officer in uniform would be a target, while a well-known nurse with a white flag would not:

'Thence I endeavoured to drive [Nurse O'Farrell] her to Boland's Mills, Ringsend. Owing to barricades across Lower Mount Street, and having tried all routes down by the river which was held by the rebels, and hearing reports of continuous firing further on, I had again to allow the nurse to proceed on foot to deliver the document under cover of the white flag'.

Max Caulfield, in *The Easter Rebellion*, page 355, writes: 'Nurse O'Farrell, a brave and lonely little figure, set off through areas where bullets still flew, carrying the instrument of surrender. She went to Boland's Bakery, where de Valera refused at first to believe its authenticity. She left not knowing whether he intended to surrender or not'. 'In the end, on the plea that only by surrendering immediately were they likely to save de Valera's life, they gave in'.' De Valera, escorted by Cadet Mackay, a military prisoner', insisted that his men follow the surrender order to the letter and marched in formation out of the bakery. 'He stopped the first respectable person he saw, Dr Myles Keogh, and informed him that he wished to surrender. The message was immediately passed on to the military'.

Captain Hitzen, the arresting officer takes up the story: 'I received information that a man in the green Sinn Féin uniform was in Sir Patrick Dun's Hospital almost opposite our Head Quarters. I went over and seeing the man, covered him with my revolver and told him he was my prisoner. I noted he was of officer rank and ascertained he was Éamon de Valera, Commandant of the 3rd Bn IRA stationed at Boland's Bakery. I asked him if his men were prepared to surrender, and he said he had come for that purpose'. Out of this encounter a remarkable friendship developed and amazingly Edo John Hitzen was made an honorary member of the Old IRA. (*Source*: Éamon Ó Cuiv, de Valera's grandson and Anne Hearsey, great-grand niece.)

Many years later de Valera joked with H. de C.-W. 'I am, you know, a lucky man.' 'Why?' asked my grandfather. 'Because all those that you arrested were executed. You could not get through to me in Boland's, and I survived!'

APPENDIX 5

THE SURRENDER MANIFESTO

A copy of the surrender manifesto with Pearse's original signature and dated by him 29th April 1916 at 3.45 pm is amongst H. E. de C.-W.'s papers in the National Library, and the original with all three signatories (i.e. Pearse, Connolly and MacDonagh) is in the Imperial War Museum London. It is therefore curious that one dated the 30th April 1916 sold for an incredible €700,000. This was reported in *The Irish Times* on 26th May 2005:

'Pearse surrender letter sells for €700,000'

'A surrender letter handwritten by Padraig Pearse at the time of the 1916 Rising has sold for €700,000 at auction-10 times its guide price'. 'The letter, dated 30th April 30th 1916, the day after the surrender, was bought by a telephone bidder from outside Ireland.' The vendor remained anonymous.

'The National Heritage Conservation Group, which had unsuccessfully lobbied the State to purchase the letter on behalf of the National Museum, made several bids for the document but was forced to retire at €95,000. The Keeper of Arts and Industry division of the National Museum said they already had two surrender documents. The article continued: 'There were thought to be four or five of these handwritten documents by Padraig Pearse which he sent to garrisons at Boland's Mills, Jacob's Factory and Church Street.'

According to H. E. de C.-W.: 'After the interview' (with General Sir John Maxwell) 'Commandant Pearse signed several typed copies of his manifesto, which was dated by himself, Dublin, 29th April, 1916. 3.45 pm'.

After H. E. de C.-W. had secured the signatures of Connolly and MacDonagh his task, with Nurse O'Farrell, was 'to communicate the orders to surrender' to the Commands at the College of Surgeons, Boland's Mills, Jacob's Biscuit Factory, St Patrick's Park, The South Dublin Union and the Marowbone Lane Distillery. Each surrender manifesto was on embossed British Army official notepaper.

Regarding Connolly's surrender H. E. de C.-W. wrote: 'Commandant Connolly dictated his own orders which I wrote down underneath General Pearse's typed orders, and this document was signed and dated 29/16 by Commandant Connolly.' He continued: 'On the following day this document was presented by me to

Commandant Thomas MacDonagh who added: 'After consultation with Commandant Ceannt and other officers I have decided to agree to unconditional surrender also. Thomas MacDonagh, Commandant. 30.1V.1916 3.15 p.m.'

The first, in the National Library of Ireland, is a draft written on cardboard by Pearse in 16 Moore Street on the 29 April.

The second, in the National Museum of Ireland, is handwritten by Pearse, and dated 29 April 3.45 pm.

The third, the official copy, is in the Imperial War Museum, London, with Pearse's message typed, Connolly's and MacDonagh's handwritten.

The fourth and fifth, in the National Library of Ireland, from H. E. de C.-W.'s papers, and de Valera's papers, are on embossed paper, both signed by Pearse beneath his typed message, and dated 29 April at 3.45 pm.

The sixth in the National Museum of Ireland, is handwritten by Pearse, for the Enniscorthy Command, dated 30 April.

The seventh, handwritten by Pearse, dated 30 April, was to get the surrender of some wild young rebels in the Four Courts command. It was this one that sold at auction for €700,000 in 2005.

The fourth to the seventh do not have the contributions by Commandants Connolly and MacDonagh that are on the official copy.

APPENDIX 6

FINDLATER'S AND THE RISING

Findlater's leading branch was in Sackville Street, now O'Connell Street, in the block beyond the Gresham Hotel, and almost opposite the Parnell Monument and Great Britain Street (now Parnell Street) where Pearse's surrender took place. The company were one of the largest grocers, wine, spirit and beer merchants in the country, with 21 branches. It is therefore amazing that it was not looted, particularly as the rebels and general population were desperate for food. Maybe it was because of the location, by the Parnell Monument and Rotunda Hospital, where the British cordon was tightening in on the rebels that saved us.

With the city in turmoil, van deliveries, Findlater's *modus operandi*, were impossible. The firm's Minute Books do not provide much information: 'Business discussed generally', they say, and the next week 'Business generally discussed'! Maybe wise in times of Rebellion!

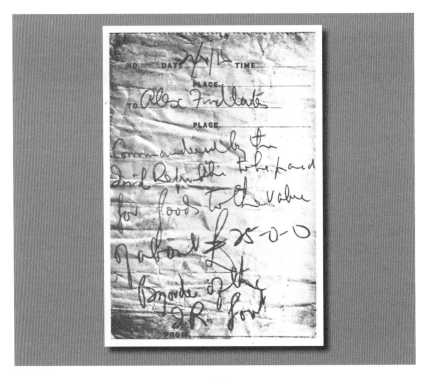

Commandeering note
Records the commandeering of foods to the value of £25 on behalf of the Irish Republic. These supplies were doubtlessly to have the GPO well provisioned. This was on Easter Monday, the first day of the Rebellion. £25 is the equivalent of €2,000 in 2015. Shops nationwide were closed on Easter Monday; the caretaking staff chose wisely to keep out of trouble and give out the goods.

Irish Times.

5.   DUBLIN. FRIDAY MAY 12, 1916.   PRICE ONE PENNY

Findlater's apologise for the inconvenience to their customers during the Rising.
(The Irish Times)

Findlater's branches were north and south of the Liffey, and there was a wholesale business through the country. The head-quarters, 28 to 32 Upper O'Connell Street, was a vast establishment, a great hive of activity, incorporating wine cellars, whiskey maturing in cask under bond (Excise supervision), beer bottling (mainly Guinness), storage of groceries in sacks and boxes, the administration and accountancy for the entire organisation, and the stabling for the dray horses for deliveries (they were out to grass for the bank-holiday weekend). In addition, the retail departments: bacon, cheese, dairy and poultry, confectionery (biscuits, bread and cakes, the latter from the firm's bakery in Thomas Street), fruit and vegetables, groceries and teas (from the firm's blending and packing premises in Rathmines) and a large wine, spirit and beer department and Tea Rooms below ground level.

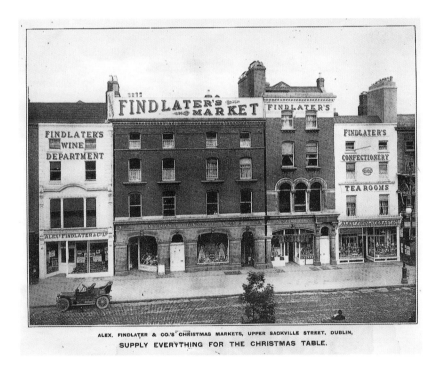

ALEX. FINDLATER & CO.'S CHRISTMAS MARKETS, UPPER SACKVILLE STREET, DUBLIN, SUPPLY EVERYTHING FOR THE CHRISTMAS TABLE.

Findlater's 28–32 Upper Sackville Street